Language Competence

THE WASHINGTON PAPERS

. . . intended to meet the need for an authoritative, yet prompt, public appraisal of the major developments in world affairs.

MANUSCRIPT SUBMISSION

The Washington Papers and Praeger Publishers welcome inquiries concerning manuscript submissions. Please include with your inquiry a curriculum vita, synopsis, table of contents, and estimated manuscript length. Submissions to *The Washington Papers* should be sent to: *The Washington Papers*; The Center for Strategic and International Studies; Georgetown University; 1800 K Street NW; Suite 400; Washington, DC 20006. Book proposals should be sent to Praeger Publishers; 521 Fifth Avenue; New York NY 10175.

The Washington Papers/119

Language Competence

Implications for National Security

Kurt E. Müller

Foreword by Vernon A. Walters

Published with The Center for
Strategic and International Studies,
Georgetown University, Washington, D.C.

New York
Westport, Connecticut
London

Library of Congress Cataloging-in-Publication Data

Müller, Kurt E.
Language competence.

(The Washington papers, ISSN 0278-937X; vol. XIV, 119)
Bibliography: p.
1. Language and languages – Study and teaching – United States. 2. United States – National security.
I. Title. II. Series.
P57.U7M84 1986 418'.007'073 85-31240
ISBN 0-275-92213-8
ISBN 0-275-92214-6 (pbk.)

The *Washington Papers* are written under the auspices of The Center for Strategic and International Studies (CSIS), Georgetown University, and published with CSIS by Praeger Publishers. The views expressed in these papers are those of the authors and not necessarily those of The Center.

Library of Congress Catalog Card Number: 85-31240
ISBN: 0-275-92213-8
ISBN: 0-275-92214-6 paper
ISSN: 0278-937X

First published in 1986

Praeger Publishers, 521 Fifth Avenue, New York, NY 10175
A division of Greenwood Press, Inc.

Printed in the United States of America

The paper used in this book complies with the Permanent Paper Standard issued by the National Information Standards Organization (Z39.48-1984).

10 9 8 7 6 5 4 3 2 1

August, Fred, Rolf, und dem Andenken Fritzens, Alberts, Ewalds, Edmunds, und Otmars gewidmet. Zu verschiedenen Zeiten in verschiedenen Uniformen unter verschiedenen Fahnen hat jeder seinem Vaterland treuen Dienst geleistet.

Contents

Foreword

We live in a time when the importance of foreign languages cannot be overstressed. Today's communications and the acceleration of transportation have made the whole world our neighbors.

Foreign markets play an increasingly important part in our business world, yet we rarely have the linguistic skills to compete with our rivals who have understood the importance of communicating with their customers. We, alas, have not.

In the struggle for the minds of men, we largely have to do so through dubbed television or else subtitles, both of which often turn off potential viewers.

For the military, the importance of being able to talk to our allies is vital if we are to work with one another and remain allies. We must no longer expect them to be able to speak English. This ability goes far beyond the field of intelligence. It reaches into human relations and enables us to forge friendships that will ripen into comradeship.

It has always seemed to me a scandal that we have had 300 thousand men in Germany for 40 years, and yet so few of them have learned to speak fluent German. I believe everyone serving in Germany and Korea should at the end of their tour be tested for language ability. If they cannot communicate, they have not been doing their part to fortify our alliances, and this should be indicated in their fitness reports. I know that there are many distractions, but these skills are of critical importance to our nations. Reserve officers should be given special credits for language skills.

When I speak of language skills, it is not in the narrow sense. It means our understanding of the culture and history of other peoples. How can we understand them if we do not know how they come to be and who their heroes are? Such knowledge vastly increases the ability to reach them and makes it easier to learn their language.

Every facility should be given to Americans to learn foreign languages. These skills are as necessary as any other military specialization in the future, perhaps more. We cannot compete if we cannot answer. Three of the five current U.S. ambassadors to the United Nations speak Russian, Spanish, Portuguese, German, and Italian. All speak French. One speaks Dutch. These skills have proved invaluable in lining up support for our position.

The U.S. language programs in general have been disastrously small. This is the time to change it, and I hope Dr. Müller's book will be widely read and its message heard. It is vital to our country's interests, and the military community can show the way by providing the right example and the proper motivation.

Vernon A. Walters
U.S. Ambassador to
the United Nations

May 1986

Acknowledgments

Every piece of writing is to some extent a collaborative work. Even in the shortest article, the author depends on colleagues for suggestions, on library and clerical staff for their various skills, and on an editor for numerous improvements to the original typescript. It follows, therefore, that the more time spent on a research project, the more assistance the author needs.

In producing the text at hand, I have a number of persons to thank. For the original impetus to research the topic, I wish to thank my colleagues Richard Brod, director of foreign language programs at the Modern Language Association, and C. Edward Scebold, executive director of the American Council on the Teaching of Foreign Languages. For their enthusiastic support in disseminating the results of my first paper on the military significance of language competence, I wish to thank Dr. Rose L. Hayden, president of the National Council on Foreign Language and International Studies, and Dr. J. David Edwards of the Joint National Committee for Languages. For their encouragement in providing reader reactions to that paper, I thank Colonel John Bloom, editor of *Military Review*, and Professor David P. Benseler, editor of the *Modern Language Journal*. My year at the U.S. Army Command and General Staff College (CGSC) enabled me to pursue the topic in far greater depth than before, and for the support of this institution I am particularly grateful. Lieutenant Colonels Winfried Barthmus and Gerd Evert of the CGSC faculty and W. Stuart Towns of the University of West Florida were not only sources of encouragement, they were also willing, but gentle, critics.

College librarians Mary Crow, Pat Javaher, and Helen Rutledge were continually willing to help, as were Joan Morgan and Rita Siebenmorgen. Librarian Dan Dorris, chief of reference services, deserves special recognition for his assistance in locating documents dating back to World War I, as well as recent information recorded on microfiche. For various types of support, I want to thank Janis Virant of the CGSC library. I have also been fortunate in taking advantage of this age of the silicon chip and integrated circuit. For their assistance in enabling me to use the college's computer facilities for text editing, I want to thank faculty Lieutenant Colonel Marvin Hampton and Major Chuck Medvitz and the staff of Roger Dreyer's Directorate of Automation, particularly Tom Barger and Edwin Haynes.

After my year at Leavenworth, I continued to seek supporting materials. The library staff at the U.S. Army War College proved to be as willing to lend assistance to me as the CGSC staff was to their students. A particular note of gratitude is due to Dr. Richard J. Sommers, archivist-historian at the U.S. Army Military History Institute, for suggesting and making available the papers of various generals as well as providing information on relevant papers and memoranda by students at the Army War College.

Finally, for her meticulous production of the final typescript, I wish to thank Jenny Ruiz-Perez.

About the Author

Kurt E. Müller is executive vice president of the National Council on Foreign Language and International Studies. He is known for addressing professional issues in the language community, for his surveys of manpower in the profession, and for work on communicative approaches to language teaching. He has taught at Rutgers University (where he received his Ph.D.), Hunter College (City University of New York), and the Defense Language Institute and has served on the staff of the Modern Language Association. A frequent speaker at professional conventions and a contributor to periodicals, he is a reader, adviser, or consultant to numerous organizations, agencies, projects, and journals. In addition to graduate degrees in language and literature, he holds a degree in political-military affairs from the U.S. Army Command and General Staff College.

1

Introduction

> . . . valid national strategy must embrace all our national resources of every kind – human, material, industrial, scientific, political, and spiritual. The armed forces are simply the cutting edge – a deterrent to hostile action in ordinary times but even when used in war, a last and desperate resort.
>
> – Committee on National Security Organization, Commission on Organization of the Executive Branch of the Government

There should be no doubt that a nation's strength lies in its capacity to meet the demands of its citizens not only to be free from want but to prosper. To facilitate prosperity, a government seeks to provide its citizens the wherewithal to produce an abundance of goods and services, to seek access to an ever wider choice of goods in the marketplace, and to secure the nation against the catastrophic loss of its standard of living. If such a definition of national security seems broad, it is deliberately so. At their best, economic, material, and human resources contribute to a society's progressive development. As a result, U.S. military strength, in this century at least, has been essentially conservative. Rather than serving as a vehicle for political aggrandizement – as in dynastic or nationalistic wars – it has sought to preserve a peaceful environment for the exercise of free international trade. Thus we have seen multiple bilateral alliances give way to pluralistic collective security arrangements. In a world characterized by increasing collective action, which at times may appear to be collective inertia, unilateral decision making has become ever more rare, and we find an ever greater need to communicate with trading partners whose needs, aspirations, and motivations may differ from our own. Thus it is that in dealing with equals, language is a tool of peace.

Lest our readers deny the necessity of multilateral action in international relations and affirm instead the U.S. role as the preeminent world power (à la "big stick diplomacy"), I hasten to cite former Commander in Chief, U.S. Army, Europe, General George S. Blanchard: "we can no longer approach the problem of the defense of Western Europe from strictly a unilateral national viewpoint."[1] Blanchard observes that we have for the first time the capability of putting a multinational defense team on the ground in peacetime and that "multinational exercises are becoming more the rule than the exception." He considers a basic element in the estimate of combat effectiveness to be people and their ability to communicate on the battlefield: "Language interoperability is the key and the base on which any operating sense of cooperation should be built. For, in the heat of battle, there will be no time to request a translation of a fire mission or go directly to a dictionary to discover what *Angriff* means."[2] Hence, Blanchard considers language to be a necessary tool of war.

So it is that language skill contributes both to peace and to war. We have seen in the private sector the effect of a lack of language competence. Consider the pen manufacturer who translated an advertising pitch that claimed the use of its ink would prevent embarrassment. Unfortunately for the company, the Latin American audience receiving the message usually attached to the word "embarrassed" not the intended notion of propriety in social etiquette but the connotation of an unwanted pregnancy.[3] In the public sector, too, we have seen sufficient evidence of the lack of language competence. On February 2, 1979, the *New York Times* ran an editorial on "The Indispensable Mr. Chi," the interpreter who accompanied Vice Premier Deng Xiaoping of the People's Republic of China on his visit to the United States. As the *Times* wrote,

> In 1972, President Nixon was able to speak with the Chinese leaders in Peking only through their interpreters. Seven years later, the humiliation – and perhaps the damage – continues on American soil.

Elsewhere I have written on the importance of language competence in strategic intelligence collection and have given examples of failure to use U.S. resources to interpret, translate, and analyze information from foreign sources.[4]

My previous study of the contribution of language skill to military effectiveness was limited to materials commonly available in the press and in openly published professional literature. In contrast, this study makes extensive use of resources that are far more restricted. Although many of the materials I shall consider in these pages have been declassified for more than 30 years, their availability solely in typescript form, including on microfilm, has not afforded them sufficient dissemination. Other sources – particularly those concerning the Korean War – have been declassified relatively recently. Still other sources, from which I quote unclassified passages, remain subject to security restrictions.

My purpose in this study is to examine historical documents to determine the armed forces' need for language skills. I shall look at after-action reports from multinational operations, at publications contemporaneous with previous U.S. overseas deployment, at memoirs, at official histories, at student papers submitted at staff and senior-level service colleges, and at various staff studies. I shall also look at the U.S. history of meeting its perceived requirements. The record of the nation's last general mobilization during World War II is particularly instructive for the variety of needs it uncovers and for the cooperation it demonstrates between the military and other sectors of the society. Our mobilization experience is germane, indeed essential, to deliberate planning for any future global calamity.

As national security can be seen both from the broad perspective of the total capacity of a society to improve the lot of its members and from the narrow view of a military reaction to an external threat of aggression, so too can language skill be employed for peace and for war. Although I would rather extol the virtues of attempts toward mutual understanding in an ever shrinking global community, it is necessary to examine the need to communicate across linguistic barriers in a sometimes hostile human environment.

The Argument for Language Competence

Perhaps no other profession outside that of diplomacy is as concerned with the relationship between a nation and its neighbors as is the military. Their common interest is not surprising, of course, to the student of armed international conflict. In his classic text on the art and science of warfare, Carl von Clausewitz writes: "der Krieg ist nichts als eine Fortsetzung des politischen Verkehrs mit Einmischung anderer Mittel" (war is nothing but a continuation of political relations with the addition of other means).[5] Whether one accepts Clausewitz's observation as realpolitik or shudders at the identification of war with politics makes little difference; it seems clear that the military as well as the diplomatic arm of any government would follow with intense scrutiny the attitudes of its neighbors toward its own actions. Both devour whatever information is available on political developments in other countries. Readers of professional military journals are presented with articles on potential forces of destabilization, military buildup by adversaries, and relations with allies. Readers' comments demonstrate their acceptance of these topics as appropriate issues for professional concern.

Our unfortuante experience has been that foreign language capability in the U.S. armed forces has been restricted primarily to one sphere of military activity. In the minds of most casual observers, the military significance of foreign language competence is pigeonholed into the category of military intelligence – strategic and tactical.

But the foreign policy of the United States has suffered severe setbacks precisely because of the inability to acquire and interpret reliable information. On December 29, 1952, an Associated Press story reported the following:

> Until the first American trained especially for Indonesian duty was assigned to the Embassy in 1949, all translating was done by natives. To please their employers, they interpreted everything to sound rosy, pro-American. But when American area and language experts began to read Indonesian newspapers and attend sessions of the National Legislature, the Embassy learned that strong communist-inspired anti-American feeling was sweeping the country.[6]

Twenty years later, some in the Department of Defense found themselves making the same mistake in Vietnam. Even if the motivation here – keeping one's job – could be discounted, the drawbacks in using indigenous personnel for such tasks still exist. The accepted practice among professional translators (those who deal with written documents) and interpreters (those who deal with speech) is to translate or interpret from their second language into their dominant language. The language profession thus emphasizes accuracy of the product – based on the reasonable assumption that the source is correct.

After the Soviet invasion of Afghanistan, the United States had the opportunity to question a defecting Soviet soldier who had sought asylum in the U.S. embassy in Kabul. We failed to exploit this opportunity, however, as no one was present on the embassy staff who could speak to the defector in Russian. Failing to communicate in Russian, the soldier tried German (the second most taught foreign language in the USSR), but his German was not very good.

In intelligence collection, the utility of knowing the language of an area of interest is not limited to strategic intelligence. In a 1953 newspaper column, journalist Harold Martin relates its tactical importance as well:

> I've spent many a harassed hour in foreign lands, blocked at every turn because I could not speak the language. That was merely inconvenience but it can lead to tragedy too. For I saw a battalion badly bloodied once because nobody could understand what an excited Korean was trying to say – that a strong Red force was lying in ambush, just beyond the hill.[7]

The acquisition and processing of tactical intelligence depends on the skill with which an interrogating team questions local civilians and captured prisoners. Without language facility, intelligence specialists are impaired in, or precluded from, the successful completion of their mission. Language ability also makes a longer-term contribution to the acquisition of area intelligence: fluency in the language leads to an understanding of the culture in which it is embedded. Without the capability to operate in a given culture, a unit or an individual will, at best, realize only limited success. At worst, an operational unit will find itself alienated from its environment.

Host country relations are of significant concern to the field commander, whether his unit is garrisoned abroad or is based in the continental United States and deploys for maneuvers. Since 1977, U.S.-based military units deploying to Europe for North Atlantic Treaty Organization (NATO) maneuvers (known as REFORGER – "return of forces to Germany") have been supplementing their battalion, brigade, and division staffs with reserve officers proficient in German. Reporting on the employment of these reservists in the 1st Infantry Division, the division's chief of staff, Colonel Isaac D. Smith, wrote that the active army was deficient in language and area expertise and that the reserve foreign area officers (FAOs) "were the cornerstone of effective Civil-Military Operations during REFORGER 77."[8] In subsequent maneuvers with different units, the use of language-proficient officers has been increased. Observers have noted that the employment of such officers has greatly improved relations with the local populace and that the army would have difficulty deploying large numbers of troops if there were no access to language and area expertise.

Damage to crops, buildings, roads, monuments, homes, and vehicles costs millions of dollars in these annual exercises. Civil-military cooperation ensures that public support does not degenerate to the point of threatening the alliance. At best, however, community relations only supplement a commander's task. Central to the commander's success is his ability to obtain intelligence, to maneuver in concert with adjacent units, and to supply his troops with matériel and subsistence.

A combat force or a tactical intelligence unit would find it difficult to determine the languages in which it needs to develop and maintain expertise. The 82d Airborne Division might as easily profit from skill in Arabic or Korean as in German. Should highly mobile units maintain fluency in several languages? In practice, this question has been answered by augmenting active units with reserves, as in NATO exercises. Several reasons exist for this reliance on the reserve components. The pool of expertise is large; the active force can draw on only those individuals with the qualifications needed for a particular mission. The active component is finding it increasingly difficult to attract and retain linguists, especially in the enlisted ranks, where most language-designated positions (LDPs) are. Finally, augmentation by reserves is extremely cost-effective. Thirty percent of Department of Defense (DOD) personnel needs are met, at 5 percent of the budget, by reserve personnel. Given the increased importance of reserve linguists, it is time to look at the training they receive to acquire and maintain their language skills.

In attempting to allocate training funds parsimoniously, personnel managers would naturally tend to keep the training requirements for specific positions to a minimum. In conducting its research on LDPs, the General Accounting Office (GAO) interviewed officers overseas who had limited or no language capability. Comments from among their interviewees holding LDPs were as follows:

> A joint U.S. Military Assistance Group officer in an S-3/R-3 LDP [Speaking, level 3/Reading, level 3]* but with no language capability, said he often has a feeling of being "left out" when using a translator. As part of the Foreign Military Sales team he makes inspection tours and observes military training to see how U.S.-provided equipment is being used. During these inspection tours, he uses a translator [i.e., interpreter] when responding to questions asked by local officials. Because of this he feels his rapport with local officials has developed slowly and his communication with them is less than adequate.
>
> An assistant air attache serving in an S-3/R-3 LDP has had no language training. He needs language ability to handle situations at local airports such as dealing with security guards, ground handling crews and other non-English speaking individuals. In addition, he needs to know the host country language in order to communicate with non-English speaking attaches from other countries.[9]

The degree to which LDPs are filled by individuals with the required skill varies from one language to the next. In some languages the compliance rate is surprisingly low. In the "defense-security" occupations, the federal government has accounted for 4,576 positions requiring facility in Russian. In a background paper for the President's Commission on Foreign Language and International Studies, James R. Ruchti of the Department of State tallied only 2,039 incumbents who possessed the language qualification required.[10]

---

*The Interagency Language Roundtable proficiency scale runs from 0 to 5, with 5 indicating an educated native speaker Level 3 indicates minimal professional proficiency.

Worse than instances of individuals in LDPs who do not have the requisite language qualification is the matter of underestimating requirements. The GAO claimed that language requirements are understated and that the systems for designating language positions are inadequate.[11] GAO investigators found positions that did not require a language but for which language facility was essential. For example,

> a regional security officer, who is in a non-LDP and does not know the host country language, is not able to work efficiently when contacting foreign-speaking individuals. The position responsibilities require numerous dealings with local police, security officials, national guard, and bodyguards of the Ambassador (none of whom speak English). The officer believed that the position should be language designated at the S-2/R-2 proficiency level. Post officials, however, have never requested that the position be an LDP."[12]

The need for capability in various languages has led to greater reliance on the reserve components. If the United States expects to rely on the reserves for language skill, it had better ask about the size of the pool of qualified personnel and about the measures taken to ensure that language skills remain current.

In 1979, the coordinator of the army's Reserve Component Foreign Area Officer Program reported a requirement of 1,703 reserve FAO billets and a shortfall of 1,224 officers to fill these positions. He estimated a mobilization requirement of 2,739 officers, for which there was a shortfall of 2,259. The army's Reserve Component Personnel and Administration Center had identified 1,100 officers whose backgrounds made them eligible for selection for the specialty; the program manager noted, however, that even if all 1,100 were selected, there would still be a shortage of 50 percent of the mobilization requirement.

In comparison with U.S. allies, the United States has a long way to go to overcome the perception of the "ugly American." In the Federal Republic of Germany, for example, all officers study English. At the Führungsakademie, the equivalent of an all-service command and general staff college, officers are exempted from the study of English if they can demonstrate suitable proficiency. Those who do are permitted to study Russian instead.[13] U.S. shortcomings in international communication skills have been recognized in several reports prepared by the GAO. In one of these, the GAO lamented:

> Our January 1973 report to the Congress addressed language requirements, training programs, and language-related staffing for several Federal departments and agencies and recommended improvement. At that time, we found that language essential positions at certain overseas locations were not adequately staffed, criteria for identifying foreign language proficiency tests needed to be improved. . . . This report notes that similar conditions continue to exist.[14]

With this information as background, let us investigate the record of U.S. language needs in the military services and the attempts to meet them.

2

The View from Within: Defense Looks at Its Own Language Needs

> . . . le "sens" de mes expressions m'échappe toujours: je ne sais jamais exactement si je signifie ce que je veux signifier ni même si je suis signifiant. . . . (the "meaning" of my expressions always escapes me. I . . . never know if I signify what I wish to signify nor even if I am signifying anything. . . .)
>
> —Jean-Paul Sartre, *L'Être et le néant* (*Being and Nothingness*)

In his monumental work on the character of human existence, the philosopher Jean-Paul Sartre writes of the impossibility of communicating with others. Sartre's concern for the full range of meaning in a statement may at first seem too esoteric in the context of this treatise, but the problem he poses is one between two persons speaking the same language. We may find it comforting to discover that English is the most prevalent foreign language in the world, but lest we assume that we can communicate easily with the 1.015 billion Asians, Africans, Europeans, and Latin Americans who are studying English, we ought to reflect on the difficulty we have understanding many of the 364 million native speakers of English, as well as those for whom English is a strong second language. In South Asia, for example, 24.8 million persons use English, but we in the United States would have difficulty acknowledging that their variety of speech is the same language used in the United States.[1] Even between the United States and Britain the difficulty in mutual understanding is sometimes great. An American seeking an apartment in Britain is likely not to find anything suitable, as the British understand the term "apartment" as denoting a single room. An American "apartment" equates with a British "flat." Similarly, if Americans ask for a "subway," we would be shown an underpass. If we find the "underground," then we shall have found the mass transit vehicle we are seeking. These differences can be amusing; they can be serious if the divergence in meaning is greater or if the actions we wish someone to accomplish are crucial to us. If we were dealing in high finance and asked a bank for a loan of a billion pounds, we are likely to be asked for a clarification. An American billion is a British (French, German, Italian) milliard. A billion may be comprehensible to a Briton, a Frenchman, or an Italian, but to a German, a billion is clearly equal to an American trillion.

In North America, English has been the dominant language since before the revolution. But the degree of dominance has varied. Although the United States has never really been a monolingual nation, the impact of minority languages has fluctuated considerably. Until World War I, the influence of non-English cultures was reflected not only in ethnic settlements and the minority language press, but also in the prominent place of language in the elementary and secondary school curriculum: in 1915, 24.4 percent of high school students were enrolled at any given time in a German class.

World War I gave each of the belligerents a good measure of linguistic chauvinism. Despite U.S. involvement in a global crisis, the United States developed a cultural isolationism that was devastating to language study. Whereas almost one in four high school students had been studying German before the war, by 1922 the figure had dropped to six per thousand.[2]

By the time World War II became a threat to the United States, our orientation toward the languages of the enemy had changed. A year before the bombing of Pearl Harbor, the navy recognized that only 12 officers were fully competent in spoken and written Japanese. Aware that in the event of war with Japan the United States would need to develop competence in Japanese, the navy embarked on a survey of civilians with a knowledge of either Chinese or Japanese. Of an initial file of 600, half had so little functional capacity in the language that they were dropped on first screening. Of the rest, 56 were chosen to receive further training and become the nucleus of the Navy Japanese Language School.

The U.S. Navy began its own instruction in Japanese in October 1941; the army's Japanese program opened its doors at the Fourth Army Intelligence School in November 1941. Both services could have anticipated the demand for skill in Japanese far sooner than they did, as four members of the Army War College class of 1926 had identified the critical state of military resources in Oriental languages: Colonel Conrad S. Babcock, a cavalryman; Commander D. E. Cummings, a naval officer; Colonel Will H. Point, a quartermaster officer; and Major Alexander Wilson, an infantryman, each contributed to a collection of Army War College General Staff memoranda that discussed difficulties that the U.S. intelligence community would encounter in the event of a war with Japan. The memoranda recommended steps to be taken in peacetime to minimize the impact of language problems.[3]

In *Language and Area Studies in the Armed Services*, Robert Matthew provides a detailed report of efforts like these to build competence in the languages of the areas where U.S. troops would be.[4] Ironically, at the same time that the War and Navy Departments discovered they needed to build up language programs, the State Department suspended theirs.[5] This anomaly offers an interesting interpretation that a nation's military forces need to understand an adversary once the diplomats have abandoned their efforts to speak with him. Undoubtedly, this orientation toward the enemy is largely responsible for the identification of language skills with military intelligence.

The intelligence community begat the large-scale military interest in languages, and this segment of the uniformed services still provides the greatest number of students for the Defense Language Institute (DLI). As early as 1955, the Task Force on Intelligence Activities of the second Hoover Commission on the Organization of the Executive Branch of the Government recommended

> That a comprehensive, coordinated program be developed to expand linguistic training among American citizens serving the intelligence effort; and
>
> That the Department of Defense expand and promote language training by offering credit toward reserve commissions to ROTC students and drill credit to Reserve personnel for completion of selected language courses.[6]

Staff Studies and Service College Papers

In 1959, the army's Office of the Deputy Chief of Staff for Personnel (ODCSPER) published a staff study on "Language Training for Officers." The ODCSPER study delineated three types of requirements for language competence among officers: to meet the needs of a specific assignment, to provide a pool of qualified personnel to meet emergency or mobilization commitments, and "to enhance our prestige in those overseas locations where our assumption of World Leadership commits us to serve."[7] These three categories are implicitly accepted by several mid-level and senior officers who wrote papers at the Army Command and General Staff College or the Army War College on aspects of the Defense Language Program.

Colonel William P. Jones, Jr., for example, writes in general of the need for language competence among officers.[8] As background material, he cites a number of works that at the time of his study were standard fare for anyone concerned with language use. Additionally, he quotes from congressional documents, he extracts a lesson from a classified study, and he relates relevant personal experiences. Jones accepts what might be called the "hypothesis of cultural imperialism": the concept that an American working in a foreign country who continues to speak English exhibits an implicit arrogance by

> expecting others to make the effort to learn his language, an arrogance that suggests we are no different from the former colonial rulers. For foreigners to make the effort to learn the local working language is to demonstrate – often dramatically – a sense of respect for the people who speak that language. To avoid the effort can sometimes be interpreted as a show of disrespect.[9]

Jones follows this citation with a supporting example from his own professional experience with the Joint Brazil-United States Military Commission. "The accomplishments of this organization," he writes, "were directly proportional to the ability of its personnel to obtain the esteem and confidence of Brazilian officers. . . . Even a slight knowledge of Portuguese produced a favorable reaction." He relates an instance of two U.S. officers discussing business in Portuguese. A Brazilian officer in their midst then remarked: "you cannot imagine how it thrills me to hear two Americans speaking Portuguese to each other. My reaction is this: if these Americans have taken the trouble to learn my language and even use it in talking to each other, they must think it important, and my country, too."[10] Having consulted William R. Parker's *The National Interest and Foreign Languages*, Jones paraphrases one of the instances Parker presents of mistranslation: that of the American reporter who, during the Indochinese war, quoted a French general as demanding U.S. aid.[11] The reporter had failed to translate the French "demander," which is equivalent to the English "ask." Jones adds another example of a "false cognate" – a word in a foreign language similar to one in the native language but with a different meaning – from his experience in Brazil:

> In 1954 the Commanding General, US Army Section, Joint Brazil-United States Military Commission, wished by means of a courteous letter in Portuguese, to recommend to the Brazilian general staff a better organization for maintenance of American-furnished equipment. The translator rendered "recommended" by a form of the Portuguese verb "recommendar." Brazilian civilians do use "recommendar" in the sense of "recommended," but in the military service it has the force of an order, just as "desire" does in the US Army.[12]

One might be tempted to conclude from this example that the general would have been better off sending a letter in English and letting the Brazilians translate it, but that would have shown the discourtesy mentioned above and also been subject to the same error by a Brazilian. In this example, we have not so much a mistranslation as a failure to perceive the connotations of a word in a particular cultural environment. The same is true of Nikita Khrushchev's "we will bury you" speech. In the context of the Cold War, the phrase is menacing. In fact, however, the Russian idiom means "we will survive you" and does not convey an aggressive attitude. The United States, however, took it as a defiant remark. The hostility that results from errors in communication may not be quantifiable, but it leads us to conjecture about the crucial nature of understanding in international relations.

One of William Jones's classmates at the Army War College, Lieutenant Colonel Cyrus R. Shockey, also considered the question of language training for the officer corps.[13] Shockey notes the problem of acquiring and maintaining competence and looks at various recurring suggestions to facilitate meeting the demand. With due domestic political perspicacity, Shockey notes that U.S. prestige abroad is insufficient reason for extensive language training within the services. The state of language competence among U.S. citizens in 1960, however, was insufficient to meet even minimal language needs, and Shockey's paper seeks to recommend solutions to the wide gap between language-skill needs and the practice of filling positions requiring these skills. Rejecting blanket requirements for serving officers as too expensive in manpower and too time-consuming for effective training management – and recognizing the ineffectiveness of voluntary, off-duty programs – he proposes incentive funding for maintaining language proficiency during assignments in which the language is *not* used. In a 1968 War College thesis, Lieutenant Colonel Hanz K. Druener recommends annual proficiency examinations for officers, who would all be expected to demonstrate their capacity to use at least one foreign language. Those scoring above a particular level (ostensibly beyond a passing score) would receive proficiency pay. Those who failed the exam "in their basic foreign language" would be expected to seek off-duty instruction at their own expense.[14]

In 1970, the incentive-pay idea appears in a professional study published by the Air War College, *Approaches to Foreign Document Translation*. The author, Stephen C. Bladey, advocates incentives for linguists to maintain and expand their proficiency. Among his recommendations is one to make available subsidized courses of advanced language study and foreign residence and travel.[15] Although the personnel management system of any large bureaucracy would naturally resist individual training programs that lack close supervision, such independent development of language and area expertise is essential for acquiring adequate background in a culture. Bladey also suggests development of a linguist reserve force.

Similar to this suggestion is one by Lieutenant Colonel Norman C. Watkins, who, in a 1968 Army War College thesis, advocated "maintaining an accurate inventory of military linguists, both active and reserve" and determining annual training requirements by comparing the inventory with an assessment of need.[16] This need has been recognized and incorporated into the plans for training FAOs. Unfortunately, training remains primarily at the planning stage.

Bladey focuses on maintaining fluency and deemphasizes the military side of personnel practices. He goes so far as to suggest a rotation of assignments between military and civilian agencies so that the linguist can continue to develop his or her professional skills – a suggestion that contrasts with the practice of alternating military specialties, only one of which requires language skill. For such a scheme to be feasible, linguists would need a separate career field, and greater use might have to be made of reserve officers who would be more likely than regulars to want to specialize in the use of the restricted range of professional and managerial skills.[17]

Shockey also recognizes the difficulty of maintaining an adequate capacity in languages that require long training programs to develop minimal fluency and notes the prevalence of this problem in meeting contingency requirements in regions with a high probability for limited war. Among his concluding recommendations he suggests that the defense community make its critical language needs known to the education sector. Moreover, he recommends that the military voice its support for emphasis on oral fluency in school language programs and for the availability in the public schools of sufficient course offerings "for the student to attain a reasonable degree of mastery."[18] His concluding recommendation, which to our knowledge has never been acted on, is to study the capacity of the reserve components to meet language requirements for contingency operations and mobilization.

In a 1963 War College thesis, Lieutenant Colonel William J. Truxal, like Jones, addresses the question of cultural imperialism.[19] He advocates schooling in a "secondary" language to shield the soldier-diplomat "from the accusation of racial or national 'snobbery.'" Truxal looks at several branches and specialties and comments on language use in these. Of the tasks normally encountered by special forces personnel, Truxal writes: "It is extremely difficult to be a teacher, or an advisor, in a foreign land without being able to communicate directly with the people in their own language. Anyone who has tried to teach even the most simple subjects through an interpreter can testify to the many frustrations and misunderstandings incurred."[20]

In a paper submitted at the Command and General Staff College in 1966, Major Katsuji Kobata emphasizes language training for special forces.[21] Kobata quotes Major General W. R. Peers, army assistant deputy chief of staff for special operations, who writes that the special forces adviser "must be equipped with three essentials and related attributes: professional competence, understanding of the people and the . . . culture in his area of assignment and the linguistic capability to communicate his competence."[22]

Like the special forces, whose expertise is oriented toward defeating insurgent military and paramilitary operations, members of military assistance advisory groups (MAAGs) and military missions are often involved in teaching U.S. tactical and operational doctrine to the armed forces of a host nation. Of these assignments, Truxal writes: "Since no training method employing interpreters is truly efficient or fully effective, it appears imperative that the US instructors be as skillful in the language of the land as they are in the special knowledge they wish to impart."[23]

Of particular branches, he advises: "Civil affairs detachments should have a thorough grounding in at least one of the local languages prior to the unit's employment in the area of interest." Noting that the use of an interpreter or translator by an intelligence and counterintelligence specialist is a practice to be abhorred, Truxal remarks:

> It is almost an impossibility for an interpreter to capture the nuances, the between-the-lines meanings which an intelligence officer actually needs for the correct evaluation of the information he is receiving.[24]

Truxal's comments on intelligence and civil affairs officers are certainly on target. Yet training for employment in a foreign theater of operations often fails to test the effectiveness of a person's language skills. If the United States wishes to evaluate its capacity for conducting psychological operations, it cannot simply write propaganda in English. The psychological operations (psyops) specialist must practice the skill using another language, but are there language-qualified superiors, or a separate agency, to evaluate it? The civil affairs officer is highly trained in a civilian profession, such as civil engineering, public health, or jurisprudence. Can he or she be effective through an interpreter? I will examine the historical record in the next chapter; for now, it is enough to note that some officers have advocated hiring indigenous personnel who speak English to serve as interpreters. Only through experience can the advocates of indiscriminate local-hiring policies be disabused of the unwarranted optimism that anyone who speaks English in addition to one's native language can be an effective interpreter. In contrast to the professional practice of translators and interpreters, who generally work from their weaker language into their dominant one, U.S. military forces have often hired local persons who speak English, and perhaps read and write it, to do just the opposite. In pursuing such a policy, we run serious risks of misunderstanding.

In a paper almost contemporary with Kobata's, Major Adrian DelCamp recommends the systematic incorporation of language instruction into officer career schooling, from basic branch courses through the Army War College.[25] Through his recommendation, DelCamp attempts to bridge the gap between a recognized need for language competence and the restrictive policy of sending only those officers for language training who have been selected for positions with documented language requirements. He quotes an article authored by the personnel managers for infantry officers that admits "the desirability for all officers to become proficient in a foreign language" but notes that officers are usually expected to acquire and maintain language competence on their own.[26] DelCamp notes that a survey of students at Fort Leavenworth revealed that language courses were high on the list of preferred electives.[27]

DelCamp's recommendation is neither new nor unique. Language education has long been advocated before officers are commissioned. Modern languages appeared in the undergraduate curriculum at the U.S. Military Academy as early as 1803.[28] We have already noted a 1955 recommendation from the Task Force on Intelligence Activities, chaired by

General Mark W. Clark. In 1978, General George S. Blanchard called for the "institution in the precommissioning environment – service academies, ROTC programs, and OCS – of required and elective language courses in the history and cultural traditions of host nations."[29]

In Congress, the House Appropriations Committee agreed that language study contributes to the formative education and repertory of skills of an army officer. The committee suggested that the assistant secretary of defense for manpower, reserve affairs, and logistics consider instituting a language requirement for recipients of ROTC scholarships. Although the Office of the Assistant Secretary considered the imposition of such a measure a deterrent to recruitment, a one-year requirement, effective in the fall of 1980, was instituted nonetheless.[30] The current administration at the assistant and under secretary of defense level apparently sees the necessity for language competence as being more crucial than previously recognized and, in response to congressional desires, is now reviewing its language needs.

During 1977 and 1978, the army conducted a major appraisal of the education and training of its officers, in which it looked at the formal and informal schooling and background necessary to perform successfully in each officer position throughout the army. The commission conducting the investigation, chaired by Major General Benjamin Harrison, issued a five-volume report covering general and special requirements from precommissioning through the continuing education of general officers, entitled *A Review of Education and Training for Officers* (RETO).[31] In its well-balanced discussion of the desirability or necessity for all officers to possess a degree of language competence, the commission notes that one general officer wrote to the study group: "Foreign language proficiency remains one of the fundamental requirements for the American army officer which is seldom addressed in discussions of his education." The commission recognizes that English is the lingua franca of multinational security planning in the West and asserts that the use of another language is often "simply a gesture of good will."

Although the commission finds "no clear and discernible operational need for all officers to be proficient in another language," it notes that building rapport with allies and foreign populations "is no small undertaking" and that "The *lack of qualified American foreign language specialists in appropriate positions* continues to place the US Army in a bad light" (emphasis in the original text). Although the study group finds a general requirement for language proficiency unrealistic, it recommends that all who aspire to become officers include in their undergraduate curriculum a minimum of two years of foreign language study.[32] The timing of the RETO proposal and its consideration by the army's chief of staff coincides with the interest expressed by the House Appropriations Committee. The result is a one-year language study requirement and a recommendation that officer aspirants pursue a two-year sequence.[33]

An undergraduate language requirement is not seen so much as developing fluency in a language as it is perceived as a valuable contribution to an officer's general background. The RETO study group finds that

> Even if proficiency is not attained, or is lost, the "study" of foreign languages does provide certain residual benefits. From contact with a foreign language and the study of a foreign culture, a student quickly learns that other people often have different perceptions of reality. Just as mathematics teaches or illustrates logical thinking, foreign languages illustrate the "illogical" thinking of foreigners. Foreign language study is, thus, one of the most direct routes out of our ethnocentric cocoon.[34]

The RETO study group thus looked at two benefits of language study: development of proficiency and exposure to other cultures. The cultural question has not been addressed adequately by the language-teaching profession, as it is generally raised by social scientists rather than by humanists. Cross-cultural communication has both tactical and strategic dimensions. At the tactical level, neighboring units in a multinational force want to be sure that their counterparts on both flanks understand the higher commander's concept of operations in the same way they do. Even when two commanders use the same language, they may differ in their application of military doctrine because of the respective military cultures to which they have been exposed. Liaison teams, which I shall consider in chapter 3 for their role in resolving language issues, are especially helpful in ensuring that allied commanders and staffs share the same understanding of a tactical mission. A major contributor to direct mutual understanding across two military cultures is the practice of a military student exchange among allied nations. The presence of officers from various nations in mid staff and senior-service colleges also helps remove the ethnocentric blinders to perceptions of collective-security interests.

Consequences and Implications

That such blinders exist is the central thesis of Ken Booth's *Strategy and Ethnocentricism*. Booth argues that as culture is a basic concept in politics and history, it must play an important role in strategy. If so, then cultural appraisals and misperceptions are also significant. Although he does not want to overemphasize the impact of misunderstanding and misperception, Booth postulates that ethnocentrism "is one of the factors which can seriously interfere with rational strategic planning," that "[s]trategists as a body are remarkably incurious about the character of their enemies and allies," that "[t]hreat assessment is . . . seriously vulnerable to ethnocentric distortion," that "[s]trategists as a profession have not accommodated, in deed or word, to the problems of conflict and stability in a multicultural world," and that "[t]he pursuit of cultural and strategic relativism is a liberating experience; it is a useful antidote to the grip of ethnocentrism, ignorance and megalogic."[35] Booth asserts the presence of two factors that militate toward making the strategist a "professional ethnocentric": naïveté about world affairs and the conformist and conservative character and upbringing of the "strategic community" in the West.[36] I shall not argue the merits of Booth's proposition; it is enough to note that his concern for avoiding such a characterization is valid.

Earlier we mentioned the existence of cultural assumptions in interpreting tactical missions. Booth extends this argument to the strategic realm. Paraphrasing Robert Bathurst's article, "The Patterns of Naval Analysis," he notes that when "Admiral Gorshkov, the Commander-in-Chief of the Soviet Navy mentions 'control of the seas,' it is assumed in the West that Gorshkov means what US naval planners mean by 'sea control.'"[37] Booth continues,

> because the Soviet Navy operates in all oceans, it is now argued that it has become a "blue-water navy", a phrase which carries very specific connotations and historical memories for British and American navalists. Because Gorshkov has called for a "balanced fleet" it is assumed that he means "balanced" in the Anglo-American sense, and this would mean that the Soviet Navy could be expected to behave offensively.

In using our own cultural definitions of various terms, so Booth concludes, "Americans have tended simply to project U.S. institutional behaviour on the Soviet Union," and we are therefore susceptible to misreading Soviet intentions.[38]

As to the acquisition of another language, a prerequisite for such cultural understanding, there are a number of excellent reasons not to rely on an undergraduate language sequence as a source of language-proficient officers. First of all, the language-teaching profession has never adopted a clear-cut, generally accepted goal of producing a specified level of proficiency (however measured) in the students taking a sequence of two to four semesters. In 1967, John B. Carroll and others measured the proficiency of college seniors concentrating in French, German, Russian, and Spanish.[39] Using the government proficiency scale (accepted by the Departments of Defense and State, the Central Intelligence Agency [CIA], and the Peace Corps), he ascertained that the reading and comprehension facility of majors in these languages was generally at level 3, while their speaking facility, as should be expected, lagged behind and was generally at level 2+. No such comprehensive study has been conducted since 1967, and no study has investigated nationally the proficiency of students undertaking a one-year or two-year language sequence. In fact, only recently has the language-teaching profession moved toward a consensus that proficiency is a valid primary goal in a sequence of courses.

With its proposal to the U.S. Department of Education and the subsequent award of a grant, the American Council on the Teaching of Foreign Languages has embarked on a program to train language professionals to use the Foreign Service Institute's oral proficiency interview on their college campuses. As colleges reconsider their curricular requirements in general education, including the reestablishment of language requirements, they are finding a growing interest among the professoriat for a language requirement stated in terms of proficiency rather than in the number of quarter or semester credits a student undertakes. The development of this new emphasis on oral facility has been a major step beyond even the reorientation of professional concern evident in the audio-lingual teaching methods that appeared in the 1950s. There is a world of difference between the expectation that reading proficiency is the only skill that can be developed if students undertake only a two-year language sequence and the advocacy of proficiency in all four language skills, to be acquired by the completion of a general-education program in post-secondary institutions.[40]

The current goal that is gaining professional consensus looks toward extensive cooperation between secondary and higher education. In the late 1970s, the Modern Language Association (MLA), with the financial assistance of the Rockefeller Foundation and the National Endowment for the Humanities, formed a group of language task forces. The Task Force on Institutional Language Policy proposed the adoption of nationally recognized performance or proficiency standards. The expectation is that students would begin to study a language in high school (or earlier) and would have their achievements recognized as a step toward meeting a postsecondary proficiency requirement. Task force proposals go so far as to recommend that

> as an incentive to language study and achievement at the secondary school level, colleges should award credit to students who meet their institutional language proficiency requirement upon entrance, provided that such students continue their study of the foreign language and culture in the next, more advanced college course.[41]

Such proficiency requirements are beginning to take hold. At the University of Pennsylvania, for example, the faculty is measuring student proficiency on the government scale in preparation for converting their language requirement to one based on proficiency attained.[42] On other campuses, other tests of communicative ability are being applied, though not always – perhaps not usually – as part of a requirement. At Indiana University, an Indiana University French Communicative Ability Test has been developed to measure the achievements of students in first-term French.[43] A number of colleges and universities are pursuing internationally recognized credentials for their students, such as the *Zertifikat Deutsch als Fremdsprache* (certificate of German as a foreign language) and the *Zentrale Mittelstufenprüfung* (central intermediate-level test) in German or the *Certificat pratique de français commerciale et économique* (a certificate in commercial French) and the *Diplôme supérieure de français des affaires* (an advanced diploma in business French) for students in third-year courses.[44] These, of course, do not equate with the U.S. government proficiency levels.

Specialty Training and Skill Maintenance

The War and Navy Departments had made use of universities in developing language skills for service members – historical examples will appear in subsequent chapters – and, undoubtedly, the Department of Defense would turn to institutions of higher education again in a future general mobilization, but for the most part the defense establishment has relied on its own language institute to meet its operational requirements.

In a student paper for the Command and General Staff College, Lieutenant Colonel Charles R. Wallis discusses problems of language maintenance encountered by graduates of the DLI.[45] Language maintenance is a major problem beyond the scope of this inquiry, but, with notable exceptions, such as Joshua Fishman's landmark *Language Loyalty in the United States* (The Hague: Mouton, 1966), concerned with linguistic minorities, and the recent volume edited by Richard D. Lambert and Barbara F. Freed, *The Loss of Language Skills* (Rowley, Mass.: Newbury House, 1982), this area of inquiry probably suffers the most neglect of any research field within the language profession. Pardee Lowe's contribution to the Lambert-Freed volume is of direct interest to readers concerned with the language skills of U.S. government employees.[46]

Although Lowe's chapter appeals primarily to language professionals, it should also interest managers of government offices that use linguists because of his comparison of maintenance and refresher programs among government agencies and an appreciation of the difficulty in assessing skill loss, which may differ among languages. Despite gaps in data and inconsistencies in record keeping, the records of government agencies provide fertile ground for research on skill loss. As such, linguists and mobilization planners should foster cooperation between these agencies and applied linguists.

The RETO study was not the first comprehensive attempt since World War II to look at officer education, and it was not the first such review to address the question of language competence. A banner year for such studies was 1966, in which two separate ones appeared, one for the army and one for the Department of Defense. The Department of the Army Board to Review Army Officer Schools, also known as the Haines Board, after its chairman, then-Lieutenant General Ralph E. Haines, Jr., found the army's foreign area specialist program "very successful" but confined to a limited number of world areas. It recommended expanding the program to include "a modest number of specialists in Eastern European countries of the Warsaw Pact not [then] included and possibly some specialists in the NATO countries." The Haines Board also noted the existence of a problem recognized by numerous critics in the last two decades, both within the Department of Defense and outside it. The board found that procedures for identifying trained linguists should be improved and reutilization tours for officers who had taken the longer DLI language courses should be increased."[47]

In the same year, the Office of the Assistant Secretary of Defense for Manpower published the *Officer Education Study*. In its consideration of language needs, the Defense Department staff divided the Defense Language Program into four instructional categories: full-time, mission-required training; part-time, mission-required training, voluntary (off-duty) training; and desirable language study (for career development). I mention this categorization here to note its similarity with the ODCSPER study's enumeration of three types of requirements for language competence and to intimate the problematic nature of such a classification scheme. Although there have been frequent recommendations to the members of the officer corps that language competence is a desirable skill, there has been little substantive support for acquiring and maintaining this skill. The authors of the *Officer Education Study*, for example, state: "Each Service . . . encourages its officer[s] to participate in the off-duty voluntary language training programs and to become proficient in a minimum of one foreign language."[48] In the next chapter, I document the need for language competence. If I succeed in convincing the reader that this skill is a bona fide professional attribute, then it should be apparent that relegating its development and maintenance to voluntary, after-hours status undermines any expectation of success.

The 1966 education study also mentions briefly the stockpiling of language skills and notes that any such attempt "would require extensive and continuing training programs."[49] Earlier in this paper I asserted that the issue of maintenance, or the attrition, of language skill is still in its infancy as a research topic for language professionals. Most would agree, however, with Richard Lambert's proposed list of "predictor variables" – those we might expect to influence language-skill attrition.[50] Among the broad categories of personal characteristics – motivation, learning context, and use – I would emphasize the latter two as areas in which there should be a body of data from governmental records.

Surveys

The matter of use is fundamental to a survey of officers undertaken in 1973 by Major Harold J. Hicks. In "An Analysis of Foreign Language Training for Officers," a misnamed, but quite useful, research paper, Hicks reports the results of a questionnaire answered by 126 of his fellow students at the Army Command and General Staff College, all of whom had studied Vietnamese through the Defense Language Program.[51] The value of Hicks's appraisal lies primarily in the comparisons made among the length of the language course, the echelon of the command structure at which the officers used their skill in Vietnamese, and the individual respondent's perception of the contribution their language study had made to accomplishing the job tasks.

Hicks categorizes the courses taken by his colleagues in five increments of length: 3–5 weeks, 6–9 weeks, 10–12 weeks, 14–19 weeks, and 44–47 weeks – the basic course at the DLI. In one respect his respondents confirm the obvious: the more they had studied the language prior to their overseas assignment, the more they used the language in Vietnam. Of considerable interest is the effect of language study on the respondents' ability to accomplish their missions. The 3–5 week courses were of least utility to this group of officers: only 36 percent of those taking the shortest courses thought their language study had a significant effect on, or was absolutely essential to, their jobs in Vietnam. Two-thirds of those in the 6–9 week courses thought their language ability made a significant contribution. Of those who had taken 10–12 week courses, 62 percent said their language skill was significant or essential; 86 percent of those who had taken the 14–19 week courses and 83 percent of those who had taken the full basic course replied that their language skills had a significant effect on job accomplishment or were absolutely essential to the performance of their tasks.

Unfortunately, Hicks did not account for actual proficiency, as measured by the Defense Language Proficiency Test, as a relevant variable. Lacking this information, his results cannot easily be compared with the various investigations undertaken by the GAO. Nor can the skill levels required by various types of positions filled by army officers in Vietnam be estimated. Because the size of his responding sample for the two longest courses (13 officers) is too small for statisticians to accept, I am also hard-pressed to offer credible interpretations of the data he presents. Despite this shortcoming, however, it seems the medium-length courses (14–19 weeks) were of great benefit to the officers who took them. Therefore, it is tempting to conclude that the shorter courses should have been extended for the participants to have been more effective on the job. Hicks's data, when categorized by type of assignment, confirm this impression, though once again the small sample precludes confident opinions.

Hicks's survey includes officers who served with special forces, as province advisers, and as combat advisers. The latter group is further subdivided by echelon: division level, brigade or regimental level, and battalion or company level. A year before Hicks submitted his paper, the Human Resources Research Organization (HumRRO) published W. R. Graham's *Survey of Military Assistance Advisors*.[52] Although the Graham survey reports data for a sizable sample – more than 300 respondents for many of the questions looked at – it omits a number of important variables and fails to cross-tabulate answers with the variables it does consider. As with the Hicks survey, the Graham questionnaire does not ask for proficiency level, as defined by the government scale, although the participants should have been quite familiar with this rating system. Moreover, there is no attempt to distinguish among types of advisory functions, and there is no analysis by country, language, or even world area. This lack of specificity is a serious shortcoming that precludes any detailed interpretation of the survey's results. It is an egregious error, in questioning the importance of competence in a foreign language, to pose the inquiry to officers serving in a country where English is an official language and then to fail to account for such a circumstance. It is amusing to discover "that host country language ability was not of primary importance in at least one country due to the fact that English was the official language of the country, or because most of the host country officers spoke English fluently." It should not be surprising that the ability to read and write a foreign language is not essential in some locations.

Even without necessary distinctions among countries, the respondents to the Graham survey are quite positive in their support for language training. "Even a moderate ability to converse in the host-country language permits the advisor to follow discussions among host-country military personnel" according to 87.2 percent of the respondents. Three-fourths of the advisers agree such ability "facilitates constructive discussion," and about four-fifths agree it "speeds and clarifies exchanges of ideas." Fully 94 percent of the advisers agree that conversational ability in the language enhances rapport with their counterparts.[53] As Hicks did, Graham asked his survey participants if the inability to use the language on the job would detract from their job performance. The larger sample in the Graham survey is not as strongly pro-language as the advisers in the Hicks group: only 47.6 percent think lack of language competence would detract from their ability to function, either seriously (30.1 percent) or moderately (17.5 percent). The strong divergence in responses to the two surveys emphasizes the desirability of information on the duty stations of Graham's respondents.

Not quite a decade before Graham's questionnaire, Alfred

I. Fiks and John W. McCrary, also reporting for HumRRO, presented the results of a survey sent to 129 officers who had served as advisers in Vietnam between 1960 and 1962.[54] The Fiks-McCrary survey is limited to Vietnam and accounts for variables in the amount of English used by Vietnamese officers, the amount of Vietnamese used by the adviser, the isolation of the adviser from speakers of English, the frequency of social contacts, and the length of time in country. Fiks and McCrary asked their respondents whether they would have become aware earlier of the most important problem on which they advised or whether they would have advised more effectively had their Vietnamese language skills been better. (Graham posed no such question.) These researchers find that the typical response is "clearly a strong affirmative."[55]

By comparing responses to other questions with this one, the authors infer that the added advantage of greater skill in Vietnamese is not so much a matter of improving the direct communication between the U.S. adviser and his Vietnamese counterpart; more important, it seems that better language ability would enable the adviser to receive and assimilate information from more sources. The advisers' attempts to use Vietnamese did contribute to the relationship between the Americans and their Vietnamese counterparts, though. Supported by the results of a Chi-square (statistical) test, Fiks and McCrary report that the U.S. officers who attempted to speak Vietnamese received a greater number of social invitations. Those officers who had spent longer tours in Vietnam, as a group, were also more likely to associate more with their counterparts, and it is this group of officers that exhibits the greatest sensitivity to matters of interpersonal communication.

On Interpretation and Translation

In their consideration of interpreters, Fiks and McCrary asked their group of advisers "What was your general feeling about the accuracy of the translations?" The answers range from "top notch" to "lousy," as follows: top notch, 9 percent; good, 31 percent; fair, 41 percent; poor, 9 percent; and lousy, 6 percent. Strangely, inasmuch as the Fiks-McCrary report reinforces the earlier findings of Fishel and Hausrath, the Graham findings on military advisers are quite at odds with the results of the earlier surveys. Graham finds

> A very high percentage (93.9%) of the responding advisors (who use interpreters) indicate that their interpreters "slightly distort" or "do not distort at all" the meanings of communications between them and their counterparts. Only 6.2% of the advisors responding considered their interpreter's distortion of communication to be "serious" or "very serious."[56]

Graham's evidence is inadmissable, as his respondents are not competent to judge the degree of distortion. Nevertheless, of the 178 advisers who responded to the question, 70.3 percent agree that an interpreter does distort the meaning, though most think the distortion is slight. Fiks and McCrary, whose evidence on interpreter effectiveness also must be taken as simply a composite of laypersons' impressions, write that the longer an adviser was in Vietnam, the more sensitive he became to difficulty in interpersonal communication.[57] If less experienced advisers had fewer problems communicating, it is more likely that they were unaware of their interpreters' limitations than that they had better interpreters.

The net effect of distortion is a reminder of the proceedings of the House Committee on Un-American Activities in its questioning of the Marxist playwright and poet Bertolt Brecht. In presenting the text of some of his works as evidence of his Communist leanings, the committee asked him if he indeed wrote the lines attributed to him. Brecht insisted on retranslating some of the content or on quoting from the original. The committee's own interpreter attempted numerous clarifications, culminating only in the chairman's comment: "I cannot understand the interpreter any more than I can the witness." The final question pursued the same absurd line of questioning. After citing several lines of translated poetry, the inquisitor asked Brecht if he wrote them. "No," he replied, "I wrote a German poem, but that is very different from this."[58] With that, he was thanked for his cooperation, and proceedings against him were dismissed. He was not asked if his meaning was distorted, or the degree to which his meaning was altered. And the committee was not competent to judge the significance of the distortion, if any.

In a student thesis written for the Army War College, Lieutenant Colonel Hanz K. Druener contradicts Graham's conclusions with anecdotal evidence. Druener argues that

> an adviser is as effective as his language capability. I have seen advisers make no effort to learn the language and depend entirely on an interpreter. In one specific instance this proved to be embarrassing and could have been more serious if not corrected. Through no fault of any individual a very important commitment was *apparently* mutually consummated between a senior MAAG official and his opposite number through the interpreter assigned to the MAAG. Fortunately the interpreter made a memorandum of record for his own file and showed it to his boss who immediately picked up the error involving several million dollars in military research and development costs which the host country was to pay for a certain item but which in translation came out in the opposite connotation.[59]

In continuing to relate the problem of reliance on interpreters, Colonel Druener asserts:

> Numerous times during larger joint conferences where interpreters were needed, it was necessary for me to step into the discussion due to improper translation by the interpreters. There were also times where I noted our officials actually permit the interpreters to control the discussions due to the fact that they had become so familiar with the subject.[60]

Druener's comments should not be considered an overzealous interest in accuracy, as he merely reinforces previous findings. In their study of language problems in Korea, Fishel and Hausrath point to the "undesirable amount of power being vested in the person used as an interpreter."[61] In noting the magnitude of the language problem in leading to the failure of civil affairs operations, these researchers reiterate the findings of C. Darwin Stolzenbach and later Secretary of State Henry Kissinger's study of civil affairs problems: that the lack of language-proficient U.S. civil affairs officers put U.S. personnel "at the mercy of their Korean interpreters." In their discussion of military police operations, Fishel and Hausrath quote from their initial interview with the Office of the Provost Marshal, Eighth Army: "The military police problem in Korea can be summed up in one word: *Interpreter*!" (emphasis in the original text).[62]

Notwithstanding the difficulty of training linguists for contingencies in underdeveloped areas (i.e., in stockpiling skills in low-density languages), Stolzenbach and Kissinger recommend maintaining a pool of such linguists because "it is precisely in these areas that indigenous interpreters will prove most unsatisfactory."[63] Not only would someone hired as an interpreter have to speak English well, but he or she would also need sufficient education to be able to understand the substance of the message being translated. We cannot assume that educated bilinguals roam the villages of Third World nations when they do not appear regularly on our own streets.

Fishel and Hausrath also ran into translation problems of their own while conducting their study. A question directed to Koreans about the use of Korean by members of the United Nations command had to be discarded when the authors discovered the translation did not convey the same meaning as their English original. (In this instance, clearer expression of the original English question would have facilitated the translation into Korean.) They also discovered that the highly rated translators had rendered "Korea" as "Chosen," the Japanese term for the country, rather than with the indigenous term "Hangook." Use of the Japanese term insulted some of the questionnaire respondents.

In a student paper considering the interpreter as an intermediary, Colonel Wolfred K. White contends that an adviser should nevertheless possess sufficient language competence to have some perception of the interpreter's ability. In a survey he conducted in December 1966 at the Army War College, "former military advisors asserted that knowledge of the local language would have enabled them to 'check' on the performance of their interpreter."[64]

Congressional Interest

The various authors we have cited here on the matter of using interpreters conclude that it is far more desirable for the principals to be able to operate in more than one language, if not with complete fluency, then at least with sufficient familiarity to know if confidence in the interpreter is warranted. The optimum use of an interpreter is related by Congressman Paul Simon in his *Tongue-Tied American*:

> In May and June of 1978, I served as one of the United States delegates to the United Nations Session on Disarmament. During the first days of the session, Foreign Minister Andrei Gromyko invited the United States delegation to meet with the Soviet delegation at their embassy. Our delegation, headed by then-Secretary of State Cyrus Vance and former Governor Averell Harriman, met them at their building, decorated Kremlin-style – plain, somewhat severe. Through our interpreters we exchanged pleasantries and a few remarks of substance also. I say "through our interpreters" because I don't believe anyone in our group spoke or understood Russian, but most of the Soviet delegation, including Foreign Minister Gromyko, spoke and understood English. It may appear to be a minor matter, but it gives "the opposition" in any such dialogue additional time to prepare for the proper reply. I wish I could enter a vig-

> orous debate on the floor of the House with those kinds of odds stacked in my favor! And yet what took place in New York City between our two delegations occurs in similar meetings over and over again (and not just with the Soviets), with Americans unable to communicate directly.[65]

Congressional interest in the contribution of language competence to national security has a considerable history in the post-World War II era. Since this discussion is oriented toward the military's own perception of its language needs, I shall not endeavor to trace the range of congressional actions since passage of the National Defense Education Act. I would be remiss, however, if I did not note that Congress has repeatedly, and almost regularly, caused the Departments of Defense and State to look at their needs for language skills. In 1973, in 1976, in 1980, and again in 1982 in response to congressional inquiries, the GAO published reports on the language needs of various agencies of the executive branch and on the programs to meet these needs. The first GAO report found that positions in which a language capability was essential were not adequately staffed, that "the criteria for identifying foreign language requirements were nearly nonexistent," that records of the proficiency of agency personnel were not current, that command language programs in the Department of Defense were neither properly reported nor adequately supervised, and that the various agencies needed to cooperate more closely. The last comment was made despite the GAO's recognition that an Interagency Language Roundtable has existed since 1955.[66]

In 1976, the GAO issued two separate reports on language training and assignments: one for the Department of State and the U.S. Information Agency, the other for the Department of Defense.[67] The 1976 reports heralded the beginning of a string of GAO complaints that the executive agencies were not adequately training their personnel. Closer inspection reveals that the 1976 reports are not entirely negative. The Department of State had temporarily raised the rate by which it filled positions with qualified personnel by lowering the qualifications for the positions.[68] But an internal review of LDPs in 1975 convinced the State Department that it needed to expand the number. The percentage of appropriately filled LDPs in the U.S. Information Agency fell by 3 percent over three years, but this dip was really a step forward, as the agency recognized its language needs and increased the number of LDPs in foreign locations. The defense establishment did not fare so well. The criteria for defining LDPs were found to be too general, the qualifications of incumbents were extremely low (only 37 percent of those assigned to MAAGs had the required language proficiency), language assets were still neither properly inventoried nor current, and command language programs were still not under the control of the single supervising agency, the DLI.

The GAO issued a report in 1978 on federal support for language and area studies.[69] But, as the report concerned Title VI of the National Defense Education Act rather than the personnel qualifications of government agencies, I shall not consider it here.

As part of the conference report on an authorization bill for the Department of State, the International Communication Agency, and the Board for International Broadcasting, the GAO was tasked in 1979 with evaluating the language programs and related personnel practices of government agencies. The resulting GAO report found that language requirements remain understated.[70] Of 28 agencies receiving the questionnaire, only the Department of Defense and four civilian agencies had formal procedures for designating positions as language-essential. These systems, mentioned earlier, were found once again to be inadequate. This report marks the third time the GAO had told Congress that the Department of Defense did not adequately fill its language-designated positions. For its 1979-1980 investigation, the GAO had the good fortune to use the data uncovered by the President's Commission on Foreign Language and International Studies, which issued its report and a companion volume of background studies in 1979.

If my repeated listing of the GAO's findings strikes the

reader as a litany, let me reassure you that some government agencies, particularly the Defense Department, have freely echoed the refrain. Anyone interested in the army's efforts to meet its language needs should be aware of the five-volume *Army Linguist Personnel Study* (ALPS), produced in 1976 by the army's Office of the Deputy Chief of Staff for Personnel. Essential reading is the fifth volume, which contains the executive summary as well as conclusions and recommendations applicable to both the active and reserve components. The linguist study acknowledges the lack of current information on language assets. Data from the Military Personnel Center show that at the time of the study there were 14,232 commissioned and warrant officers and 18,500 enlisted personnel who had language qualifications noted in their records. Of these, 84 percent of the officers and 73 percent of the enlisted personnel had had their last test before July 1973, despite the requirement for biennial testing promulgated in 1969.[71] Two 1973 surveys by the Military Personnel Center had found a similar pattern of failure to comply with requirements for testing: of a sample of officers, only 18.8 percent had been tested within the two years prior to the survey, 54.3 percent had been tested more than two years prior, and 26.9 percent had never been tested. Of a sample of enlisted personnel, 40.9 percent had been tested within two years of the survey, 24 percent more than two years prior, and 35.1 percent had never been tested.[72] The ALPS implicitly recognized the difficulty of filling LDPs under a system of frequent rotation or progression of assignments. It recommended a training factor of 2.4 persons for each position.

One of James R. Ruchti's background papers for the President's Commission on Foreign Language and International Studies reports that a review of personnel records of the officers and enlisted personnel on active duty revealed a "margin of 50 percent above present requirements in most languages. The real value of this talent is debatable," he notes, "if one considers its availability, the problem of the retention of language skills, and the currency of the records which keep track of it."[73]

In a background paper written for the RETO study group

(a year prior to Ruchti's paper), then-Major James R. Holbrook reasons that "although the number of officers currently carried as possessing foreign language capability appears adequate to meet stated requirements, the level of proficiency among many of these officers is suspect and in all likelihood is not sufficient."[74] Indeed, if the percentage of obsolete proficiency ratings is still at the level of the 1973 survey by the Military Personnel Center, then a 50 percent surplus becomes a 76 percent shortage for officers or a 59 percent shortage for enlisted personnel. Among his recommendations, Holbrook includes continuing support for command language programs, establishing high priority for the development and production of language-maintenance packages, and requiring cadets and scholarship recipients to take a minimum of two years of foreign language during their undergraduate years.

Holbrook's recommendation that cadets pursue study of a foreign language was accepted and promulgated by the RETO study group, as I indicated earlier. The interrelationship between the education community and government agencies concerned with national security is an important one that I shall explore in greater detail in chapter 5. Indeed, the thrust of the report issued by the President's Commission on Foreign Language and International Studies is directed toward the contribution of the education system to national security, with "national security" defined in the broadest possible sense. During the year of the commission's deliberations, the defense establishment was surprisingly low-key in developing ties to the academic community. Perhaps the memory of campus opposition to U.S. military involvement in Vietnam kept the two from appreciating their common interests. Perhaps the decline of language study on the college campus – and its limited effectiveness – prevented rapprochement. A background paper prepared by the DLI for the president's commission pointed toward the decline of academic language study as a retardant influence on its own programs, but little else was produced for the commission that properly appreciated the historical tie between these two segments of

U.S. society. Since the commission report, however, there have been continuing developments. The deputy directors of both the CIA and the Defense Intelligence Agency (DIA) have testified in Congress in support of a bill to foster language study in the nation's schools and colleges. As Admiral Bobby R. Inman, of the CIA, testified in 1981,

> We . . . believe that such programs as the Department of Education's International Education and Foreign Language Studies-Domestic Program and the Translations Program of the National Endowment for the Humanities made substantial contributions toward solving our language problems. The Humanities Endowment Translations Program provides significant support to the Intelligence Community through translations that contribute to an understanding of the history and cultural achievements of other cultures.[75]

Similarly, in his statement before the same committee, Major General Richard Larkin of the DIA, discussing various factors that had been limiting the U.S. national capability in the use of other languages, concluded

> the availability of language-trained personnel for the defense intelligence community is shrinking while potential information resources around the globe have rapidly increased, requiring a significant addition of professionals with foreign language skills. Additional language-trained personnel in defense intelligence will also mean further improvement in the quality of our analysis through greater insight into foreign cultures.

In his summary, Larkin speaks of

> the general benefit likely to accrue to the United States as a result of increased public awareness of problems affecting other nations and cultures. In addition, such an increase in language and area knowledge would be a significant factor in developing public understanding and

> support for such national security concerns as our foreign economic and military assistance objectives.[76]

In view of the widespread distrust of the intelligence community that is often evident on college and university campuses, Larkin's statement deserves wide dissemination. It would go far in defusing academic suspicion of the defense sector.

3

Historical Need for Language Skills

> We cut nature up, organize it into concepts, and ascribe significances as we do, largely because we are parties to an agreement to organize it in this way – an agreement that holds throughout our speech community and is codified in the patterns of our language. . . . We are thus introduced to a new principle of relativity, which holds that all observers are not led by the same physical evidence to the same picture of the universe, unless their linguistic backgrounds are similar.
>
> – Benjamin Lee Whorf, "Science and Linguistics"

It is not my purpose in the present chapter to write an apologia for the acquisition and maintenance of facility in a foreign language. Rather, I shall investigate historical examples of the need for such competence within the military services.

Literacy in more than one language has long been appreciated and at times has been demanded of an educated populace. Because the English language by no means enjoys a monopoly in the publication of knowledge, it is highly advisable to read professional literature in other languages as well. In U.S. military affairs, access to such material has been recognized as valuable as long ago as 1800. In that year, President John Adams advocated the acquisition by the secretary of the navy of a library of Dutch, English, French, and Spanish works on naval architecture, navigation, gunnery, hydraulics, hydrostatics, and mathematics and of biographies of distinguished foreign admirals.[1] Toward the end of the nineteenth century, the professional study of military art and science achieved comparative dimensions with Emory Upton's travels across Europe to study the organization and training of European armies. That the use of other languages was necessary to acquire greater knowledge of military developments is evident in the early work of the Office of Naval Intelligence (ONI). The first director of that office, Lieutenant T. B. M. Mason, has been described as a linguist who, with the assistance of a small staff, increased the availability of information on naval developments by translating foreign-language publications.[2] By 1902, a considerable volume of translations was being produced on a regular basis for the Office of the Secretary of the Navy, the Bureau of Navigation, and other bureaus of the Department of the Navy.[3]

World War I

In our twentieth century experience, this largely academic need for language skill has often been supplanted by a more immediate need to communicate with allies or to intercept information from an enemy. Although we are most familiar with the extensive training begun during World War II, it might be expected that there are numerous other episodes that have required language ability, as every war the United States has fought in this century was a coalition war. In World War I, for example, the U.S. Army seems to have been concerned with the acquisition of facility in French. According to Major General James G. Harbord in *The American Army in France 1917–1919*,

> the Commander-in-Chief [General John Joseph Pershing] stated simply that he had been designated to go to France in command and desired me to go with him as Chief of Staff. Our conversation soon disclosed that I

> did not speak French, a fact not in my favor for the General himself was none too fluent in that language. I had served fourteen years in the Spanish-speaking possessions and had thought that in learning Spanish I was equipping myself for any foreign service that might occur for our Army in my time.[4]

Later in his memoirs, Harbord describes the particular contributions of a half dozen officers (some of whom later became general officers, including William Mitchell of air corps fame) who were well acquainted with the organization and tactical doctrine of the French army and who all spoke French.[5] In a published collection of letters to his wife, Harbord refers to daily instruction in French for U.S. officers aboard the troop ships sailing for Europe. He notes that instruction given by Major Robert Bacon, former ambassador to France and later secretary of state, was most popular and that the officer in charge of instruction, Colonel Alvord, was a former French instructor at West Point.[6]

In the last chapter, I mentioned the incredible drop between 1915 and 1922 in the number of students of German in U.S. high schools. Such a phobia against things teutonic is also notable in the chauvinistic propaganda presented to U.S. soldiers under the guise of education. Despite such slanted presentations, an excellent opportunity was afforded the doughboy to learn French and British history and other academic subjects through the educational programs established by the Young Men's Christian Association (YMCA). German culture, however, which had been accorded high respect in the United States during most of the nineteenth century, was suddenly transformed into an object of enmity, a taboo subject, while French became the most popular subject. John Erskine, professor at Columbia University and, in July 1918, acting director of the YMCA's educational department in the American Expeditionary Force (AEF), estimated that 150 thousand soldiers were studying French while stationed abroad; three months later, as chairman of the Army Educational Committee, he upped his estimate by 50 thousand.[7]

Reports indicate that only some classes in the instructional program were free, however. The Office National des Universités et Ecoles Françaises proposed offering courses for any group of 20 or more men who were near a large town and wanted to learn French. These courses would be taught by lycée and school teachers at a small charge of 50 centimes per person per hour. In many camps, charges for French instruction were reported to be "high": two francs per hour for soldiers and four francs per hour for officers, "but even at these relatively high rates several scores of students [were] enrolled."[8] So important was the study of allies' languages that a Commission de l'enseignement des langues vivantes dans les armées alliées (Allied Commission for the Teaching of Modern Languages) was formed with a French general officer as its president. These courses and a lecture series on British and French culture were provided to improve the fighting effectiveness of the U.S. soldier by making him "much more sympathetic with his French and English allies" and to familiarize him with the "true character, the political and social ideals which have dominated them, and the difference between these and those of imperialistic Germany."

Although these citations illustrate the official rhetoric behind the lecture program, it is more likely that the popularity of the French courses was due to far more pragmatic motivations on the part of soldiers who wanted to make themselves understood among comrades-in-arms and among the civilian populace. Harbord's memoirs do not delineate the reasons for the officers' desire to learn French, but it is clear that there were both military and social motives for doing so. At the individual level, U.S.troops had to learn to use the equipment furnished by the French. French manuals on the employment of weapons, tactics, and liaison between combat arms were translated for U.S. use. At the tactical level, U.S. regiments were supervised or assisted in their training by French divisions. The employment of U.S. units was a matter of considerable discussion, as both the British and the French wanted to use U.S. soldiers as individual replacements or to insert small units into existing commands. For both military and political reasons, Pershing, the War Department, and the Congress wanted to maintain national identity and to preserve or create the integrity of U.S. divisions and corps. At the operational level, Supreme Commander of Allied Armies in France Marshall Foch did not command in English. Even prior to this appointment, communications with French commands (e.g., at corps and army-group levels) and from the French military mission to the AEF were in French.[9]

In stark contrast to the documentation from World War II, there seems to have been little emphasis on language training for the acquisition of intelligence or for the preparation of an army of occupation. Perhaps there is no evidence of the need to teach German because enough Americans could speak and understand it. Not only was German the most commonly taught modern language in U.S. schools, but German-Americans were the largest ethnic minority.[10] Whatever the reason that facility in German was not a matter for concern, it is clear that there was emphasis on the acquisition of intelligence. A provisional intelligence manual mimeographed by the AEF outlines the composition of a divisional intelligence section and specifies the inclusion of four translator-interpreters. Such a staff might be used in the interrogation of prisoners of war; it might also be used to translate documents. Although information on specific languages is sketchy, the AEF intelligence manual asserts that

> [t]he Intelligence Section with all bodies of troops must be prepared to handle data in German, French and other languages. This requires that persons connected with the Intelligence Service as translators must be able to read not only ordinary printed data, but script, often indistinct, and be familiar with dialects and technical terminology.[11]

A printed *Provisional Combat Intelligence Manual* specifies that the interpreter staff will consist of one first lieutenant, one second lieutenant, and two sergeants. Language facility is not specifically identified for intelligence duties at regimental or battalion level.[12]

Presumably because of the acquisition of a great number of officers with little prior military experience, the AEF established a General Staff College at Langres. From the notes to one of the lectures, intelligence sections seem to have existed at every level from General Headquarters (GHQ) to regiment. At GHQ, the section dealt with strategic as well as tactical intelligence, and therefore language facility was necessary. For corps level, the lecture notes explicitly delineate the tasks to be accomplished by three officers with a command of German. Aside from examining documents and cross-examining prisoners, they were to acquire information on such items as enemy order of battle, tactics, morale, disposition, and combat service support.[13]

Prisoners and captured documents were not the only source of information requiring language skills. The introduction of indirect-fire artillery, which could be placed out of sight of the opposing forces, required fire-control measures that did not rely on a line of sight between infantry and artillery command posts. Field telephones were used for this purpose and to communicate between trenches. Before long, a way was found to intercept the enemy's telephone conversations. This source of information gave birth to the Telephone Listening-in Service, which required "thoroughly trained personnel . . . conversant with the enemies' languages not only in its [sic] scholastic form, but in the various patois, technical language, current slang, and official abbreviations."[14]

World War II

The U.S. entry into World War II was preceded by a period of mobilization, during which the U.S. government had sufficient time to consider the personnel qualifications of U.S. service members. As early as December 1940, then-Lieutenant A. E. Hindmarsch brought the lack of qualified Japanese linguists to the attention of ONI. After consultation with the director of naval intelligence and with the chief of naval operations, steps were taken to rectify this deficiency by training junior reserve officers in Japanese. During the war in the Pacific, it was necessary to translate numerous captured documents, some of historic interest, others of immediate operational significance. In 1942, for instance, a marine raiding party to Makin Island returned with air defense plans for all Japanese-held Pacific islands. When the heavy cruiser *Nachi* was sunk in Manila Bay, it provided the navy with annotated charts of mine fields and defenses, with fleet operations plans, and with materials on Japanese naval doctrine.[15] By the end of June 1944, the supply of captured war diaries, field manuals, code books, and other documents filled 130 cases, necessitating continuous expansion of the translation section of ONI. The translating unit of the Far Eastern Section alone grew from a staff of 15 to 35 by May 1944, to 65 by September, and to 95 by February 1945.[16]

Of course the navy exploited the capture of documents in the European and Mediterranean theaters as well. The invasion of Sicily in 1943 progressed rapidly enough that the Sicilian headquarters of the Italian navy was captured before the Italians could destroy their files. Documents showing the entire disposition of Italian and German naval forces in the Mediterranean, with charts of mine fields and safe conduct routes, fell into Allied hands. In June 1944, the capture of the U-505 yielded code books and tactical publications. By the war's end, ONI had translated hundreds of thousands of documents from 22 languages, and 60 percent of their work was for naval bureaus other than ONI. In eight months in 1945, more than 146 thousand documents were translated from Japanese alone.[17]

According to the linguist Mario Pei in *Language for War and Peace*,

> [s]triking examples of the way in which linguistic training can be put to military uses appeared in the early days of the war, when German parachutists came down in Holland equipped not only with Dutch uniforms but also with a command of the Dutch tongue, and German motorcyclists, disguised as French soldiers, swept across

> Belgium and northern France spreading disorder and panic in excellent French.[18]

A search of military documents related to language use has not disclosed any such dramatic evidence of deception in U.S. operations. The bulk of the material concerns the identification of problem areas and the efforts undertaken to resolve the difficulties encountered. The army's experience during World War II determined the necessity for language-qualified personnel in numerous military specialties, which is similar to current requirements. Although I have not discovered any cross-tabulation of skills (such as the number of personnel trained in engineering who could understand Chinese), the narrative descriptions of the Army Specialized Training Program confirm the obvious expectation that such combinations were needed. As with demands for other specialized training, such as in communications or in chemical or mechanical engineering, requests for language-trained personnel varied widely from one six-month period to the next, sometimes from one quarter to the next. Although production and demand records often do not agree when sources of information are compared, the need for language skills is well documented.

Major users of linguistic skills were military intelligence and the Office of the Provost Marshal General. Records concerning military intelligence reveal significant emphasis on the development of skill in Japanese. Because the historical records of various school programs assert that curricula remained responsive to needs articulated from the field, developments in the curriculum were an indication of the tasks to which linguists were to apply themselves.

The Military Intelligence Service Language School (MISLS) and its predecessor, the Fourth Army Intelligence School, taught general language skills, such as translation and interpretation, oral expression, and reading and writing. Japanese military commands, interrogation of prisoners of war, geography, and Japanese field regulations were added and dropped as dictated by the needs of field units. Additional training was necessary for some graduates of the MISLS program: some were to meet U.S. Army Air Force intelligence requirements, others were to acquire order-of-battle information on the Japanese army and navy at the Joint Intelligence Center, Pacific Ocean Areas (JICPOA), at Pearl Harbor. MISLS had access to classified material direct from the field, which not only made it possible to work with fresh, authentic materials, but also to identify emerging needs before they were officially recognized by the War Department.

Counterintelligence operations, specifically in censorship, provided a sizable requirement for Japanese linguists. A communication between Admiral Chester W. Nimitz, commander in chief, U.S. Pacific Fleet and Pacific Ocean Areas, and the commanding general of U.S. Army Forces, Central Pacific Area, established the magnitude of the censorship effort. In response, the director of intelligence, Army Service Forces, estimated Nimitz's requirement to be "about 2,000 officers and men in addition to several thousand U.S. and Japanese civilians." Of this total, 256 were to be "expert linguists."[19]

Signals intelligence during World War II was a Signal Corps responsibility, as it had been in World War I. In a recent article in *Army Communicator*, Major Richard Riccardelli surveyed the use of electronic warfare and signals intelligence in supporting ground operations in North Africa and Europe. Agreeing with John Hixson and Benjamin Franklin Cooling, authors of *Combined Operations in Peace and War* (Carlisle Barracks, Penn: USA Military History Institute, 1982), Riccardelli concludes that "[p]erhaps the most significant factor in U.S. mobilization in support of the Signals Intelligence field was the lack of language-qualified personnel." Moreover, Riccardelli finds the current requirement for linguists remains crucial and that research and development to automate word and phrase recognition will not substantially diminish the need for linguists.[20]

Civil Affairs and Military Government

The temporary substitution of military authority for civil government suffers from a long tradition of misunderstanding. Commanders at the tactical level have little exposure, if any, to questions of governing civilians in their areas of tactical responsibility. Except for the contributions made by local resources to the execution of a mission – providing transportation or items peculiar to the environment, repairing roads, and the like – the commander finds the presence of civilians in a combat zone a time-consuming nuisance. Even at the theater level, a commander finds the civil responsibilities thrust on him a burden to be borne only so long as absolutely necessary. In the opening paragraph of their history of civil affairs during World War II, Harry Coles and Albert Weinberg quote a letter from the supreme commander to the army chief of staff:

> The sooner I can get rid of these questions that are outside the military in scope, the happier I will be! Sometimes I think I live ten years each week, of which at least nine are absorbed in political and economic matters.[21]

General Dwight D. Eisenhower was not the first U.S. commander to deal with civil affairs. The imposition of military government in an occupied area had been fraught with argument in every conflict from the Mexican War to World War I.[22] The U.S. aversion to military rule could easily lead the military to relinquish control of an occupied area before it is secure. Indeed, several executive departments can claim, and have in the past claimed, interest in administering an occupation government. Coles and Weinberg present extracts from numerous documents, illustrating, for example, the interest of the Department of the Interior: "because of this Department's unique experience with primitive people, we should participate actively in the administration of any island in the Pacific which may be occupied and governed by the United States."[23]

The secretary of war had requested from his cabinet colleagues recommendations of individuals who might receive commissions direct from civilian life, officers who might become available to these same civilian agencies after the necessity for military government had passed. One of the historical reports of the Military Government Division of the War Department relates the reaction of the other departments: "The smoldering antagonisms to War Department leadership in the occupational program burst into flame. Two entire Cabinet meetings were devoted to a debate on the matter in October and early November 1942."[24] In some sectors, fear of military control was expressed in writing by government officials:

> The civilians are in danger of losing the postwar world by default. They are in danger of losing out because they seem to lack a comprehensive plan and a unified purpose. The Army, on the other hand, has a plan and a purpose. The Army's plan is to train administrators for the postwar world and thereby to control it.[25]

Such fears could well have been based on writings familiar to the military. The Clausewitzian dictum that war is a continuation of political relations can certainly be interpreted as advocating the usurpation of powers over the assets of another sovereign nation. But even in countering aggression, the employment of military force entails assuming control over civilians. By default, a commander assumes responsibility for the welfare of the inhabitants of his area of operations. His responsibility is grounded in international law through the annex to Hague Convention No. IV, embodying the Regulations Respecting the Laws and Customs of War on Land (1907) and further recognized, after World War II, in the Geneva Convention Relative to the Protection of Civilian Persons in Time of War (1949). Like it or not, the commander is tasked with continuing to provide the services of the defunct government, from food supply, to public hygiene, to education. Eisenhower's task was not unique except in its magnitude. His message traffic with the War Department shows the theater commander's potential for exercising foreign policy. If control is returned to local politicians, particularly to those returning from exile, the commander in effect sanctions a new regime. If he relinquishes control to a civilian agency, he jeopardizes his logistic lines of communication. If he retains control, he must impose administration by a full-time civil affairs staff.

At the policy-making level, too, military government was an unpopular concept. In a memorandum to the secretary of war, President Franklin D. Roosevelt expressed his concern that "the governing of occupied territories . . . is [primarily] a civilian task."[26] Despite jurisdictional disputes, the War Department planned, even prior to U.S. involvement in the war, for military government by an occupation force. In a directive from the G-1 to the provost marshal general (PMG), dated December 3, 1941, the PMG was given the mission of training officers for detail to military government activities.[27] In responding to the directive, War Department planners discovered the United States had been involved in occupation operations since the Seminole War but that the government had never trained a single officer for such duties. Estimates were made of occupation forces used by other countries. Initial investigations revealed that the German occupation of Belgium in World War I required 3,500 troops and that the existing Gouvernement Générale in Poland numbered at least 7,000.[28] Most useful to the PMG was the discovery of the after-action report filed by the chief civil affairs officer of U.S. forces occupying the Rhineland after World War I. In it, Colonel I. L. Hunt laments the lack of qualified personnel assigned to occupation duty. According to the Army Special Staff history of military government, Hunt "closed that report, almost with a prayer, that never again should the American Army be permitted to undertake such a task without having first trained a sufficient number of officers qualified for the work in those special duties that were involved."[29]

To its credit, the War Department recognized that officers assigned to occupation duty "must know something of the habits, customs, thinking and reactions (and preferably the language) of the people upon whom they are to impose military control."[30] By June 1942, only a month after the first class began, the Provost Marshal General's Office (PMGO) recognized the competition from the civilian agencies in the government and requested authority to expand its fledgling training program.[31] By September, the School of Military Government, which had been established at the University of Virginia, began to prepare surveys of requirements for civil affairs officers for Germany, Italy, and Japan; the surveys were later extended to areas of potential occupation. In October and November, the PMGO received authority to offer reserve commissions in the Army Specialist Corps (a technical branch that now exists only for selective service cadre and for chaplains prior to their ordination) to 2,500 civilians. To augment the School of Military Government, an additional course was established at Fort Custer, Michigan. Graduates of the Custer program then proceeded to 1 of 10 universities at which Civil Affairs Training Schools (CATS) had been established.

As civil affairs requirements grew, of course, so did the training programs. The Custer program began with authorization for 100 officers per class and by September 1943 was up to 450. CATS, too, expanded from a group of 6 universities to 10: the original participants were Harvard, Yale, and Stanford Universities, the Universities of Chicago, Michigan, and Pittsburgh; the expansion added Boston, Northwestern, Western Reserve Universities, and the University of Wisconsin. Students in the program at the School of Military Government, which was oriented toward Europe, included Public Health Service and Medical Corps officers, U.S. Navy and U.S. Marine Corps officers – the navy also had its own CATS – and 43 officers from allied nations.

I have related the fear of civilian agencies that occupation government would be too militarized. In fact, this did not occur, as few career officers possessed the qualifications the Military Government Division was seeking. Of 9,180 officers whose records were submitted by the Classification and Reassignment Branch of The Adjutant General's Office, 676 were accepted by the Military Government Division selection board. Of these, only 128 eventually entered the program.[32] As various functions were to be filled by civil affairs officers, differing selection criteria are to be found in the after-action reports of the programs. According to one section of the PMGO paper, each student was expected to come to the program with considerable experience at the managerial level in his field, and it was "highly desirable that Civil Affairs officers have some knowledge of the language" of the area in which they would serve. Professional or administrative skill was the primary selection criterion to which language skill was subordinated in anticipation of the successful employment of the intensive language-instruction model advocated by the American Council of Learned Societies.[33] Another section of the same paper claimed that officers "with real acquaintance with certain foreign countries were especially desired, and language qualifications, administrative or executive ability, and personal qualities of high order were other important factors considered in the selections by the Provost Marshal General."[34] ("Other" refers to a primary criterion of "exceptional distinction" and "particular success" in technical or professional fields in civilian life.) The School of Military Government and the CATS programs differed in emphasis: the school was oriented toward staff work; CATS was oriented toward field operations. Consequently, "language instruction . . . and the study of foreign peoples and foreign areas [were] to be a most important feature of instruction in the CATS, whereas [such study] had been definitely subordinated to other instruction at the School of Military Government."[35]

The civil affairs officers who were expected to work with the local population apparently made good use of their newly acquired language skills, if we judge by an unsolicited letter directed to the Yale CATS:

> For many months now I have been meaning to drop you a line, just to let you know that your efforts to prepare us for Italy have borne rich fruit. My work in the field of Agriculture brings me in contact with many of Class I Yale men and I think you have a right to feel satisfied with the way they are putting your lessons into practice. I, for instance, recently made a thousand mile swing through Southern Italy, encouraging the production of

> next year's crops – without an interpreter. Others of the group are sitting as judges in allied courts trying civil cases, or handling the ever difficult problems of supply. Many of us are, of course, in Southern Italy, where by their own admission, they are a bit backward. But thanks to the language and background courses I have been able to discuss "Latifundium" over the dinner table with the owner of a 20,000 acre barony without (knowingly at least) stepping on pet corns or creating acrimonious arguments. Had it not been for the sympathetic and accurate interpretation of Italian life and characteristics I very much fear for the outcome of a discussion of such a touchy subject.
>
> So when you sometimes wonder (as all humans do) whether or not the job of creating the correct skills and impressions in the first class at Yale was really worth the wear of doing well, just reread this, and other letters I know you must have received, and be of good confidence – for we're not letting you down.[36]

Of the graduates of European-oriented courses, 1,714 were sent to the European Theater of Operations (ETO). Plans for civil affairs in the Far East called for training successive six-week classes of 250 each at the School of Military Government; graduates would then proceed to one of the CATS for six months' language and area training (and additional military government subjects). The army sent an additional 350 officers to the Navy School of Military Government at Princeton University.

Korea: Language Needs Never Met

One of the worst instances of our national lack of language competence occurred during the U.S. participation in the Korean War. Intelligence requirements and civil affairs problems encountered in previous U.S. experience abroad arose again in Korea, but this time with additional difficulties. And this time the United States found a major gap – far worse than in the U.S. experience in France in 1917 – in the command and control structure of the UN Command.

That the U.S. government underestimated the magnitude of U.S. language problems in Korea can be seen in the reports of no fewer than four observer teams sent from the Office of the Chief, Army Field Forces, in Eighth Army documents on linguist policy, in a major study by the Operations Research Office (ORO) of The Johns Hopkins University, and in historical files on interallied operations.[37] The observer teams noted repeatedly the inadequacy of trained interrogators. Team No. 5 found there was a "great need for personnel trained in proper techniques of interrogation." Observer Team No. 6 commented on the adequacy of both training and personnel: "In numbers, the interpreters and linguists are too few. All need a reorientation with stress on the Oriental psychology. . . . [Most are not competent] to interrogate without indigenous interpreters." Observer Team No. 7 reiterated this complaint, adding further deprecatory details: "Most of the interrogations and translations are being carried on by Chinese nationals and indigenous Koreans. . . . about 20 percent of the required Korean and Chinese-Mandarin linguists needed in FEC [Far East Command] are being trained."

The ORO research team reports the existence of four levels of linguist skills, labeled A through D. At the bottom of this scale, Class D linguists, which might tentatively be equated with level 2 on the current scale, were used in the signal, military police, medical, ordinance, quartermaster, and transportation corps; in handling prisoners of war; in supervising local labor forces; in some advisory assignments; and in combined operations with UN units. Class C linguists, which from the ORO description may be roughly equivalent to level 3 (minimum professional competence), were needed in intelligence, civil affairs, and advisory groups, and among military police. Class B linguists were to be found in intelligence, psychological operations, civil affairs, in advisory groups, and in the attaché system, handling POWs, in criminal investigation detachments, in the Army Security Agency, and among the military police. Class A linguists were considered in a "super" category; these were accomplished professionals with specific skills, such as simultaneous interpretation, that are beyond the characteristics of a level-5 speaker of English and another language. For these linguists, the ORO report mentions tasks of advising and negotiating, as at the peace talks at Kaesong and Panmunjom, and laments that "the Army has no career personnel in this category in either Korean or any Chinese dialect."[38]

Wesley R. Fishel and Alfred H. Hausrath, the ORO authors, point out the qualifications of the interpreters at the peace talks. The principal Chinese interpreter for nearly two years was First Lieutenant Kenneth Wu, USAR, who received his commission specifically for his work as a language officer. His replacement, in 1953, was Lieutenant Colonel Robert B. Ekvall, USAR, who was called to active duty for this express chore. The principal Korean interpreter was Lieutenant Horace Underwood, USNR, a missionary who served at the peace talks until July 1953. He was replaced by an army noncommissioned officer (NCO), whose lack of rank made negotiating difficult – "not so much in dealing with the enemy across the table, but in dealing with U.S. negotiators."[39]

At the highest level of proficiency, the linguist also has a thorough familiarity with customs, habits, social psychology, and cultural anthropology. On one occasion at Panmunjom, for example, Lieutenant Wu noticed that the ears of the Chinese delegates grew red during a presentation by North Korean General Nam Il. The indication was that the Chinese disagreed with Nam's position, and this information proved advantageous to U.S. negotiators. On another occasion, Wu overheard Chinese General Hsieh Fang whisper in a Chinese dialect other than Mandarin – one that had not been used during the talks – that the Chinese held a particular hill. The hill in question was held by a UN unit at the time, but the general whispered "we'll attack tonight and take it, and by tomorrow morning it'll be ours anyway."[40] The UN units were thus warned of the impending attack and were reinforced, although not sufficiently to hold the hill against a heavy Chinese advance. These highly professional skills require constant use in context to maintain a keen edge. Both Colonel Ekvall and Lieutenant Underwood, whose language skills were of high caliber, noted that they had considerable difficulty initially in meeting their tasks.

The lack of language-qualified interrogators resulted in the need to use interpreters in up to 90 percent of all interrogations. The common pattern reported to the ORO research team

> was for a Japanese-speaking interrogator to question a Chinese POW through a Korean interpreter who understood both Japanese and Chinese (reminiscent of the classic rumor experiment of psychologists). The reason for this complicated, cumbersome, and unsatisfactory procedure was the inability of most interrogators to interrogate without the aid of indigenous (intermediate) interpreters and the corollary inability of most qualified linguists to interrogate effectively.[41]

Psychological operations required linguistically qualified interrogators, interpreters, translators, script writers, calligraphers, announcers, monitors, and observers. But in 1953, the Eighth Army psychological warfare division reported that the lack of acceptable proficiency among U.S. military linguists compelled the Eighth Army to use indigenous personnel for these purposes. Responsibility for the correct and appropriate translation thus fell to Korean Critical Military Specialists (CMS) and Formosan Department of the Army Civilians (DAC). The shortage of language-qualified U.S. military personnel meant that

> [p]ropaganda materials once written in English and translated to the Korean or Chinese could not be checked for accuracy, clarity, intent, content analysis; the American personnel never knew whether or not the desired information, message, or effect was being gotten across to the target audience.[42]

Any translator could tell us that a good translation is

actually a recreation of an intended message, and any educated bilingual can affirm that an idea conceived in one language is far more easily developed in that language than translated into another. Not only did the lack of qualified U.S. personnel risk inaccuracy in U.S. propaganda efforts, it also offered the potential security risk of a willful mistranslation. To check the accuracy of translations, scripts and broadcasts were monitored in Tokyo and Washington, but only after the fact.

In the scramble for scarce language resources, there is an understandable penchant for hiring local personnel who have at least minimal facility in English. In Korea, the United States made use of 1,800 Korean army officer-interpreters and numerous enlisted personnel and civilians. Of 228 Korean civilians working for the U.S. Eighth Army in June 1953, 100 were subject to induction into the Korean army. The Eighth Army G-2 considered this situation serious:

> The loss of these civilians would seriously cripple division, corps, and Army POW interrogation, as well as counterintelligence and communication reconnaissance activities. The Department of the Army has been able to furnish only a small fraction of Korean-speaking intelligence personnel. It will be impossible for Eighth Army to fulfill AFFE [Armed Forces, Far East] post-hostilities intelligence requirements if CMS personnel are lost through induction.[43]

Prudence dictates that hiring personnel whose primary allegiance is to a country other than the United States poses a security risk. And such risks were encountered in Korea. For example,

> On 20 Nov 52 an interrogation of a Chinese Communist POW conducted for 302d MISC by a Chinese DAC, formerly an officer in the Chinese Nationalist Army, brought to light the existence of an underwater tunnel, presumably under the Yalu River. Reportedly this was the initial mention of this tunnel; the information was

evaluated as fairly reliable, and insofar as was known this remained the only report on the tunnel. But on 9 Mar 53, "Periscope," a copyright feature of *Newsweek* magazine, published a brief report that Nationalist Chinese intelligence had learned of the existence of a tunnel beneath the Yalu River, and phrased it in terms similar to those of the mentioned interrogation report. Officers in the office of ACofS, G2 [assistant chief of staff for intelligence], Eighth Army, drew the conclusion that the contents of the interrogation report had been leaked to Nationalist Headquarters in Formosa by the DAC who had conducted the interrogation. This could not, of course, be confirmed, but the inference is reasonable.

In another instance, a Korean translator-interpreter employed by the 302d MISC was apprehended in April 1953 by the CIC [Counterintelligence Command] in Seoul after having been accused by another Korean of being the head of an intelligence gathering net and of supplying the accuser with a forged 302d MISC pass. It was eventually ascertained that the accused translator not only was employed by the 302d MISC but simultaneously also by 8240 AU. Subsequently, significant discrepancies were noted in the content of captured document translations performed by the accused for 302d MISC, one document containing NKPA [North Korean People's Army] APO numbers (which he omitted from his translation), another outlining the organization and operation of an intelligence net. The latter document was reported by the accused to be "unintelligible due to poor handwriting." However, subsequent investigation by 302d MISC revealed the second document to be clearly written. Ultimately, he was discharged by both U.S. intelligence organizations that had employed him.[44]

Command, Control, and Communications in the UN Command: The Use of Liaison Teams

Current U.S. foreign policy commitments lead the military planner to envision an operational environment that is multinational. Military doctrine, as espoused in Field Manual 100-5,

Operations, devotes attention to regional security arrangements in Europe, Korea, and Japan. Common to U.S. operational capacity in all three areas is concern for command and control, coordination and liaison, combat organization, environment, and language. The role for command and control relationships foreseen for these areas is to maintain the integrity of large units under national control. This arrangement was not what the United States had in Korea, however.

Aside from the U.S. and South Korean divisions, combat, support, and service-support forces were contributed by 20 countries, as follows:

- Belgium: one infantry battalion and one infantry detachment from Luxembourg
- British Commonwealth Division (formed from units already in Korea on July 28, 1951):
  - Australia: one infantry battalion
  - Canada: one infantry brigade
  - India: one field ambulance and surgical unit
  - New Zealand: one artillery battalion and a service corps unit
  - United Kingdom: two infantry brigades
- Colombia: one infantry battalion
- Denmark: one hospital ship
- Ethiopian Expeditionary Force: one infantry battalion and support elements
- French UN Command: one infantry battalion and additional staff elements
- Greece: one infantry battalion
- Italy: one Red Cross hospital
- Netherlands: one infantry battalion
- Norway: one mobile ambulance and surgical hospital
- Philippines: one battalion combat team, including one artillery battery, one tank company (without tanks), one reconnaissance company (seven tanks), and one replacement company
- Sweden: one Red Cross hospital (mobile evacuation)
- Thailand: one infantry regiment of one battalion with medical and military police detachments and support elements

Turkish Armed Forces Command: one separate brigade with artillery and combat support, combat service support elements
Union of South Africa: air and naval forces

This paragon of international cooperation was not without its difficulties, to be sure. The typical employment of the UN units, as the non-U.S. units were called collectively by the U.S. command, was by attachment of a UN battalion to a U.S. regiment. Because U.S. personnel constituted the bulk of the UN force, orders and directives were issued in English, with the burden of translation falling on the supporting UN unit.

The use of English in this context should not be viewed as cultural imperialism. In a paper written for the U.S. Army War College, Colonel Wallace Wilkins cites Britain's Field Marshal Sir William Slim, who in a 1952 address to the U.S. Army Command and General Staff College, asserted: "Staff procedures of a large allied headquarters should be that of the commander – of his nation . . . and I think the same of the language."[45]

In the UN command, problems of understanding differed greatly among units, from extensive difficulties in the Turkish brigade and the French battalion to minimal difficulty in the Colombian battalion. At the first major action in which the Turkish brigade took part, at Kunu-ri against the Chinese, the Turks suffered losses of 20 percent in killed, wounded, or missing in action. Losses in communications and vehicles were first estimated at up to 90 percent (later revised slightly downward); only six artillery pieces were salvaged.[46] The blame for this debacle was placed on misunderstandings resulting from language differences. As a consequence of this action, the Turkish Armed Forces Command (TAFC) was detached from the Second (U.S.) Division and attached instead to the 25th (U.S.) Division. Through the use of liaison teams of English-speaking Turkish officers, much of the language difficulty was overcome. The Turkish brigade sent liaison officers to adjacent regiments, and the 25th Division sent an advisory group to the brigade. Additionally, the assistant division commander often accompanied the brigade, and his presence contributed to improved understanding between the two units. The TAFC commander and his G-3 attended commanders' conferences whenever possible and dispatched English-speaking liaison officers to each echelon up to division headquarters. In a letter on the topic of working with UN forces, Captain Richard Harwell notes a disadvantage to the use of liaison officers: "a Turkish junior officer's interpretation of orders was only commensurate with his language capacity and familiarity with U.S. tactical concepts."[47]

Communications with the French battalion were complicated by the structure of the French UN Command. (Several allied force contributions were encumbered by the presence of national command elements to which the combat unit was subordinated while operationally commanded by a U.S. force.) Although a French liaison officer was attached to the 23rd U.S. Infantry Regiment, "all orders and official contacts had to be conducted through the French liaison officer at regiment and by personal visits to the French UN staff." The insistence on such a chain of communications retarded the battalion's reaction to commands from the regiment.[48]

By contrast, the Colombian battalion had relatively few problems in understanding orders from the regiment to which they were attached. They had sent an advance party to the UN Replacement Center to translate U.S. regulations, manuals, and directives, and they found assistance in this task from Puerto Ricans in the 65th U.S. Regiment.[49]

Other UN units had relatively little difficulty understanding the U.S. command. All the officers and most of the NCOs in the Dutch battalion spoke English well, though the commander of the regiment to which the battalion was attached made a special effort to ensure complete understanding. Similarly, most Belgian and Ethiopian officers spoke English, but again U.S. commanders made extra efforts to ensure that orders to the Belgians were explicit.

This evidence shows that language difficulties between allied forces can be overcome by attaching bilingual liaison teams to at least one of the units. Let us look at the extent of the attachments and at the problems the U.S. command encountered in adopting this solution to difficulties in communication. The Greek battalion received two Greek-speaking U.S. officers and was attached to the Seventh Cavalry Regiment at least partly because one of the U.S. battalion commanders spoke Greek. The regiment reported that one of the officers handled administrative and logistical matters and remained with the battalion executive officer. On the operational side, the regiment reported that the U.S. liaison officer and the Greek commander became inseparable. An additional Greek-speaking U.S. officer was assigned to the regimental operations section to facilitate communication with the battalion. Further support was provided by Greek-speaking U.S. enlisted personnel attached to the Greek motor pool and to the mess and communications sections. In response to a questionnaire, however, the regimental commander noted that the language barrier was a serious obstacle and that the battalion did not remain in continuous communications with the regiment. The command pointed out that the Greeks' reluctance in this area resulted in a lack of fire support at a critical time.

It was not always the case that the Greeks enjoyed bilingual liaison teams, as the description just given, culled from Major William Fox's volume, *Inter-allied Co-operation during Combat Operations*, might lead us to believe. In his 1968 student thesis, written for the Army War College, Lieutenant Colonel Hanz K. Druener looks back at his own experience with the Greek battalion. In an operation in which the Greek battalion was to relieve Druener's battalion in place, the two units discovered that none of their staff officers could communicate in the other language and that no bilingual officer was available from the next higher echelon. Details were coordinated

> by having the Greek battalion commander relay to his S-3 who spoke German. The Greek S-3 relayed to me and I in turn relayed to my battalion commander in English. This continued back and forth until the relief

> was completed. To this day I shudder to think what was lost in the translation.[50]

The Dutch and French battalions received U.S. liaison officers for artillery, armor, and mortar support and for access to the Tactical Air Control Party. They, in turn, sent liaison officers to their respective regiments. The Belgian and Philippine battalions supplied liaison officers to the Third U.S. Infantry Division, a dispatch that was probably in addition to liaison with the supported regiments.

The Ethiopian battalion sent two English-speaking officers to the 32nd U.S. Infantry Regiment, one to work with the intelligence staff and one to work in operations. Liaison was also established with the division. In after-action comments, the commander of the Ethiopian Expeditionary Force asserts: "We had no difficulty of language worth to be mentioned in dealing with American units."[51] As it was, and is, extremely unlikely to find Americans capable of speaking and understanding Amharic, the battalion took care to have at least one English-speaking Ethiopian officer on a patrol, regardless of its size, if the need for fire support was anticipated.

Although liaison with the Colombian battalion posed no problems because enough U.S. officers and enlisted personnel spoke Spanish, the liaison teams were taken from within the personnel ceiling of the parent command. As the liaison element consisted of one officer for the battalion, one enlisted man (EM) per staff section, two EMs per rifle company, and one EM for the heavy weapons company, the loss of personnel was significant. As smooth as operations in this battalion seem to have been, command and control were indirect. As the adjutant of the 21st U.S. Infantry Regiment reported, "During tactical operations orders are issued directly to the U.S. liaison officer, who in turn gives them to the unit commander. This considerably reduces the effect and impact of the orders."[52]

Most of the units considered here have been allied battalions in support of U.S. regiments. The Turkish Armed Forces Command was large enough to receive attachments of U.S. units, and the Turks received U.S. units placed under operational control of, or in direct support to, the brigade. In this event, the Turkish command furnished the U.S. commander with an English-speaking liaison officer so that in case a unit had to call the brigade for fire support, the interpreter could transmit the call.

The use of effective liaison teams was essential to the command and control of multinational units in Korea and such teams were employed extensively. A request from the Thai battalion for permanent attachment of U.S. advisers for the maintenance of vehicles and weapons seems to have led to a review of the liaison system. Because personnel billets were not provided for advisers, considerable paperwork began to flow between headquarters, ending with a study by G-3, Eighth U.S. Army, Korea, that recommended additional billets be provided by the Department of the Army. The result of the interchange was that UN battalions were to be authorized one field-grade and one company-grade officer and a driver with a jeep and trailer. UN brigades were to be authorized one colonel as senior adviser, three field-grade and two company-grade officers, and six drivers with jeeps and trailers. Not all these positions were filled, as the Belgian, Canadian, and Colombian commands never received their full complement of advisers.

Communications provided a considerable challenge to the UN command. With the exception of the Commonwealth Division, UN units used U.S. signal equipment. But equipment was not abundant. When the Turkish and British brigades were attached to a division, under the guideline that higher level units provide communications to subordinates, the division signal company found it had to stretch its existing resources to cover an extra brigade without augmentation by additional personnel or equipment.

The use of various signal nets is of some interest. The Dutch, whose officers and NCOs spoke English, had no difficulty in communicating. They used English on the regimental net and Dutch within the battalion net. The French requested radio operators for their end of the regimental net.

Because these operators did not speak French, they passed messages to interpreter-translators who, in turn, forwarded them to the addressees. The Belgian and Greek battalions were furnished U.S. radio operators, and the Colombian battalion received bilingual switchboard and radio operators from the 21st U.S. Infantry Regiment. The Filipino battalion provided its own English-speaking switchboard operators.

Communications and fire-support arrangements were not at all standard. In some cases, communications were rather cumbersome. In the case of the Republic of Korea (ROK) Army, which had a shortage of English-speaking personnel, close air support was called in through ROK forward observers to a ROK fire direction center, where the Tactical Air Control Party had a representative. A ROK artillery officer would translate the call for close air support and then forward it to the American Tactical Air Control Party.

Problems in intercultural communications, in overcoming a language barrier, and in providing logistic support differ by command level.[53] Brigadier General Thomas L. Harrold, deputy commander of the First U.S. Corps, asserted that the language barrier was not a serious problem to overcome.[54] On the other hand, at the regimental level, Colonel W. A. Harris noted that "The language barrier is a serious obstacle and plans to overcome it must be made immediately."[55] And Colonel W. C. Bullock, commander of the Second Division Artillery, wrote: "Language barriers were never completely overcome."[56]

In the discussion of the need for language skills during World War II, I considered the impact of military operations on the local population and the amelioration by civil affairs teams of the destruction of a society's economy and public services. The need for such teams was recognized in Korea and resulted in a structure under which corps and divisions were augmented by civil affairs staff for planning and monitoring, while a Korean Civil Assistance Command was responsible for field operations. I shall not investigate anew the effectiveness of civil affairs operations but shall simply accept the findings of previous studies on the topic. Both the study of civil affairs in Korea by Stolzenbach and Kissinger and the Fishel and Hausrath study of language difficulties in Korea attribute the failure of civil affairs operations largely to the linguistic incompetence of the teams. Stolzenbach and Kissinger find that civil relief efforts were subject to graft.[57] Contracts, according to Fishel and Hausrath, "customarily included a provision for 10 percent 'droppage' – i.e., 'squeeze' or graft. Ostensibly because of ambiguities of meaning in translated explanations, the Korean officials involved originally interpreted this to mean that 10 percent could be extracted as 'droppage' at each stop en route to a destination!"[58]

As none of the civil affairs officers in the U.S. Eighth Army spoke Korean (and only one spoke Japanese), such results are not surprising.[59] Extensive use of Koreans, hired as interpreters through local labor offices or available through the Korean army or the national police, did little to alleviate the problems encountered in trying to communicate with the Koreans. Fishel and Hausrath report that a civil affairs team chief discovered several weeks after delivering a major address on the occasion of Sam Il Chol (Korean Independence Day) "that his speech had been badly misinterpreted by his *best* interpreter" (emphasis in the original text).[60]

Even when the interpreter is competent, cultural factors may militate toward falsified translation. In some instances it may be that the answer itself, rather than its translation, is false. If so, then familiarity with cultural proclivities may tip us off. Fishel and Hausrath relay such a suspicious circumstance:

> I was traveling through ______ Province, checking on the distribution of rice during the previous month. I became suspicious of the answers my interpreter was relaying to me. So I asked, through the interpreter of course, whether the particular mayor I was talking to had received (1) the Cadillac automobile and (2) the mink coat KCAC had sent him. In both cases the reply was a very grateful affirmative.[61]

The authors imply that the mayor was giving a response he

thought would please the American. Unfortunately, we are not told how the team chief dealt with the cultural proclivity for pleasing the power base at the expense of honesty.

Fishel and Hausrath distinguish between civil affairs and military government assignments, although the two areas are treated similarly historically and the qualifications for such assignments are alike. The authors feel that the interpreters used for military government assignments should be U.S. military linguists, particularly because U.S. security interests must be represented before foreign officials.

Language choice in liaison assignments with the host country's government takes on political significance. Although Japanese could often be used pragmatically for its value as a lingua franca in the region, acceptance of Japanese as a medium of communication differed according to the status of the government official. At the lower strata, the United States could effectively use Nisei (U.S. citizens of Japanese ancestry) to communicate with many Koreans; about 70 percent of the Korean population was reputed to have some facility in Japanese. President Syngman Rhee's open animosity toward things Japanese severely limited the effectiveness of the Nisei at higher strata, because of course the Nisei are racially Japanese though American citizens. Although the use of Japanese at the lower and middle strata of Korean society might be interpreted as exhibiting an interest in Asian affairs, it could be taken as an affront at the higher strata. The ORO authors report that high government officials, political leaders, and Korean army officers above the rank of colonel objected to speaking Japanese with Americans.[62] The use of Japanese was one more indication that Americans valued their Korean allies less than their previous enemies: Japan was a popular rest and recreation site, indicating the greater desirability of Japan; many officers' messes were closed to Korean guests; and U.S. latrines were off limits to Koreans. The use of Korean, on the other hand, was well received, as indicated by this quote from a high Korean official educated in the United States: "When I hear on those rare occasions an American express himself in Korean, I forget he's a foreigner! It does not matter that he is not fluent. He is trying!"[63]

Although their responsibilities are quite different, civil affairs and military government personnel are historically linked with the military police, perhaps as much because of the frequent contact these individuals have with the inhabitants of an area as because of the genesis of civil affairs through the PMG. The Eighth Army Provost Marshal's office had a great need for Americans capable of speaking Korean. As one field-grade officer in the provost marshal's office told the ORO researchers,

> *First* we need those [interpreters] that understand everyday conversation but need not speak well. They should be Caucasian-Americans, and capable of dissembling so as to pick up information without seeming to be aware of the conversation they're listening to.
>
> *Second* we need those that speak fluently and understand equally well. Ideally, these too should be Caucasian-Americans. But realistically, Korean-Americans or first-rate indigenous are probably the best now available.[64]

A good portion of the concern for acquiring U.S. speakers of Korean was based on matters of operational security. Fishel and Hausrath cite one military police officer with four years' experience in the Far East: "The efficiency of the military police program could be doubled if the interpreters were loyal to us." As another officer, in a criminal investigation detachment, noted,

> The interpreter is permitted to see only that part of a case which is to be translated. Even Mr. ______, who has been with the ______ since 1950 and is reliable can't be trusted on security matters.
>
> U.S. linguists would make the work of CIDs far more efficient and far better integrated than now is the case.[65]

Through numerous such examples, the ORO research team shows how unfamiliarity with the language and culture contributed to inefficient operations and undesirable results, while some degree of language skill facilitated police work. Investigators at the scene of an accident, who could ask questions of witnesses and understand their answers, could save days of searching by documenting on the spot the names, ages, and addresses of witnesses. Monolingual investigators without good interpreters are reported to have turned prisoners over to the Korean national police "for kicking and beating" to obtain the desired information.[66]

Among the responsibilities of the military police is the administration of POW compounds. The ORO team documents many of the problems that the POW Command had to face in running compounds for Chinese, for Communist North Koreans, and for anti-Communist North Koreans. Aside from the obvious need for language-proficient interrogators and translators to acquire timely intelligence from prisoners and captured documents, the administration of a POW camp requires an ability to safeguard the prisoners: the Geneva Convention of 1949 embodies the principle that captivity is intended as a form of protective custody under which the combatant is precluded from further participation in the war. The safety of prisoners depends to a great extent on the ability to communicate with them. The ORO team reports that the lack of interpreters hampered efforts to separate accused war criminals from the witnesses to their alleged crimes. Asian interpreters were extremely vulnerable to attacks by the prisoners, and the need to protect them from prisoners exacerbated the lack of language-proficient Caucasians. The shortage of U.S. interpreters

> frequently made it impossible to explain to POWs that they were wanted for questioning – not for killing or torture; that if they would come out they would not be harmed. As a consequence, many prisoners would be called out by guard personnel, would attempt to flee in terror from the guards, whereupon the guards then

> would go after them and (in the case of Korean guards, particularly) beat them or, in a number of instances, kill them, to prevent their escape.[67]

Such tragedy hardly requires further comment.

This kind of blot on U.S. history stands in sharp contrast to the laudable efforts the United States had made during World War II to familiarize European and Asian POWs with U.S. society. The same attempt was made in Korea. As many of the North Korean and Chinese prisoners did not want to be repatriated after the armistice, they were schooled in academic subjects so as to enhance their chances for success in South Korea or elsewhere. Because the United States did not have its own teachers capable of presenting information on the United States, however, it used Formosans in selling the United States to the troops of the People's Republic of China. The teachers had never been to the United States and were ineffective and inappropriate representatives of North American society. Academic subjects, such as Korean history, geography, and the sciences, were presented by prisners and monitored by the Asian interpreters. None of the supervising Americans was able to understand the discussions in these classes.

Between Korea and Vietnam

> White House
> Washington, D.C
>
> February 15, 1963
>
> MEMORANDUM FOR THE SECRETARY OF DEFENSE
>
> One of our Military Social Aid[e]s to the White House is about to go to Laos as an Assistant Military Attache. I do not want to interfere with his assignment, but I find this morning that he has only a very limited knowledge of French. I do not see how he could be effective

> in Laos without knowledge of the language. I would think that the Army might have many officers who have language facility.
>
> I would like to receive a report on whether Attaches are expected to have a language facility in French or Spanish before they are sent to countries where these languages are spoken. I do not think we should expect an Attache to pick up the language upon his arrival there.
>
> Would you let me have your thoughts on this.
>
> JOHN F. KENNEDY[68]

President Kennedy's memo to Robert McNamara is an important artifact; it documents a stage in U.S. communication with the inhabitants of countries to which it sends diplomatic missions. The Foreign Service Institute had opened its doors only 16 years before Kennedy wrote this memo.[69] Prior to that time, foreign service officers undertook language training "on a personal basis, if at all, resulting in the frequent dependence on interpreters or on the possession of English skills on the part of foreign nationals."[70] As I shall show in the next chapter, the record of language training by military officers is not as dismal as this comment on the diplomatic corps might imply. The commander in chief's concern for the effectiveness of an official representative of the U.S. government was certainly well intended, and it is typical of the early 1960s. Today we might criticize any attempt to train an attaché in the language of the colonial power rather than in the national language: as we have shown in the matter of using Japanese in Korea, local reaction to the use of the colonial language can shift with the prevailing political winds. Seven years after the Kennedy memo, Howard Reese writes of the choice between Arabic and French in his *Area Handbook for Tunisia*:

> The choice between Arabic and French can reflect a political orientation, an attitude toward religion or a stand in the contest between modern and traditional

> values. When a conversation in Arabic reaches a certain level of technicality, the speaker must switch to French. Bilinguals talking in French about uncontroversial matters change to Arabic if the conversation touches on emotional or controversial subjects or if the speaker becomes agitated.[71]

Writing in 1979 on "French as a World Language," Jesse Levitt looks at the question of language choice in a number of francophone countries. Of Morocco, he writes that the Istiqlal Party "has asked citizens not to pay utility bills if they are worded in French and has called on businessmen to do their paperwork in Arabic."[72] The selection of language used in bilingual societies and organizations is a complex matter with numerous variables, and we shall not consider it in this study. It is sufficient to note that the question has been raised and that access to facets of a particular culture may remain blocked without the capacity to use the language(s) of that culture.

Peacetime military uses of languages tend to concentrate on the acquisition and dissemination of information. To observe the military activities of a foreign nation effectively, an attaché must understand the information available through open sources like local and national newspapers and magazines. Reliance on the English-language press without access to radio and television news reports would severely limit the effectiveness of an attaché.

The dissemination of U.S. military knowledge and the transfer of advanced technology to Third and Fourth World nations is far more effective when accomplished through a common linguistic medium than when encumbered by the time-consuming process of interpretation or translation. In response to an inquiry on language and area expertise, Major General T. J. Conway, chief of the Joint U.S. Military Advisory Group to Thailand, writes in a letter to Brigadier General Henry C. Newton: "As you know, the educated Thais all speak English. . . . If we didn't leave Bangkok, our requirements for Thai would be minimal." But advice is not, nor should it be, imparted only to those who share our language. Conway observes: "difficulties arise in the field at the lower advisory level – regimental commander and below. . . . to 'get to the troops' Thai language facility will always be required."[73]

In a paper on the use of foreign languages in naval psychological operations, Gerald C. Bailey takes a step back from the subject of his inquiry to look at psychological factors in communicating with foreigners. The primary objective for a Seabee Training Advisory Team, for example, may be to train members of a foreign naval force in the use of U.S.-built equipment. Although the use of the appropriate foreign language may generally be seen as secondary, Bailey concludes that it

> may be clearly required owing to the nature of the mission, the lack of interpreters or the difficulty in performing the mission with an interpreter. . . . careful analysis of these missions would probably reveal that wherever the conveyance of information is important, the acceptance and use of the information by the foreign national is critical to U.S. interest.[74]

Bailey finds that the adviser's purpose is not simply to communicate information, but, more broadly, to influence behavior. Denigrating the view of language as simply a tool for communicating information, he asserts that the "behavior of the foreign national is affected . . . by the total communication process and not just by the words of the intended message."[75] Citing psychological studies, Bailey implies that authoritarian character traits are counterproductive in seeking to influence the behavior of others. If authoritarianism "indicates a lack of social sensitivity . . . rendering the individual less able to deal effectively with the needs of others," then an "integrative orientation" – skill in (cross-cultural) interaction – is central in achieving the cooperation of another, whether it be to reveal information in an interrogation, to succumb to propaganda, or simply to develop a positive disposition toward the United States and its representatives.[76] Any interference between two individuals will reduce the effectiveness of attempts at communication between them. Aside from at least doubling the time necessary for instruction in using equipment, the use of an interpreter may well interfere with the rapport that should be established between an adviser and the troops he is to train. As Bailey asserts,

> [a]nother significant difficulty with the view of language as a tool is that it tends to ignore the effects of use of a language on the foreign national. In reference to the instruction on weapon employment, the way in which language is used may have a great deal to do with the motivation of the foreign national to learn about the weapon and how he will use the weapon at some time in the future, in addition to other attitudinal effects.[77]

The comments of Howard Reese and Jesse Levitt on the use of French, cited above, are applicable here to English. If the need for interpretation keeps distance between adviser and trainee, the latter may never accept the behavior the trainer intended to instill in him.

Contingency operations, such as in Lebanon, Berlin, Grenada, and the Mayaguez affair, often involve short-term insertion of a military force to recapture an asset, to maintain lines of communication, to rescue a threatened population, or to maintain peace among feuding parties. Where the local language is not English, it is clear that assignment of personnel proficient in the local language should clearly be an asset. This capacity is valuable not only in purely military operations, but in relief actions as well. In August of 1964, for example, Hurricane Cleo devastated the southern coast of Haiti. Through the U.S. embassy in Port au Prince, the Haitian government requested assistance from the United States. Within hours ships from the Amphibious Ready Group were off the coast of the island and were ferrying landing parties to Les Cayes airport by helicopter. The U.S. Marines were not met by either Haitian officials or representatives of the

U.S. embassy, however; they were, instead, surrounded by elements of the Haitian Army. After naval and marine officers failed to communicate their peaceful intentions in English, one marine officer was able to recall enough French to convince the Haitians that the U.S. Navy landed by invitation and was not there to threaten Haitian sovereignty. The tension soon lessened and the remaining wait for government officials was considerably more comfortable.[78]

Vietnam: Lessons Learned from Korea, Lessons Ignored

As with every war the United States has fought in the twentieth century, military operations in Vietnam were undertaken on a coalition basis. Allied troop commitments peaked between 1966 and 1969. The leading allied contribution was provided by South Korea, whose 10 battalions in 1966 were raised to 22 the following year and remained at that level through 1970; Korean troop strength reached 50 thousand in 1968. Thailand gradually increased its force contribution to six battalions in 1969, with a 1970 peak in personnel strength of 11,586. Australia reached its high point with three battalions in 1968–1970, with a personnel ceiling of 7,672 in 1969. The Philippines contributed as many as 2,061 persons in one year, the Republic of China sent 20–31 per year from 1964–1970, and Spain sent up to 13.[79] According to Generals Larsen and Collins, requests for military assistance from allies were subject to several areas of consideration:

> The first . . . was a unit's ability to contribute favorably to the progress of the war, with immediate and noticeable effect. Other problem areas were command and control, security, areas of operation, linguistic barriers, special situations engendered by nationality, religious customs, degree of acceptability in South Vietnam, and the donor nation's ability to house air units.[80]

About half the factors thus required language and area knowledge. During the Korean War, the United States had found that religious customs and national cultures directly influenced logistics, as cultural preferences and habits determined the acceptability of particular foods for various supported allied units. Because the United States was supplying subsistence for UN units, it had to adjust meal planning to eliminate pork for Islamic troops, beef for Hindus, and to substitute rice for bread for Filipinos and Colombians.

Larsen and Collins report that liaison between Koreans and Americans was quite good:

> Since all of the senior Korean officers and many of the junior officers spoke excellent English, they had no difficulty in communicating with the Americans, and their understanding of U.S. ground tactics made it easy for the forces of the two nations to work together.[81]

Larsen and Collins note that there were initial difficulties between the Koreans and the Vietnamese troops because of the language barrier.[82] Civil support for the presence of the Koreans seems to have been quite good, however. General Chae, the senior Korean commander, deliberately brought the Koreans and Vietnamese closer together. Working with Vietnamese government officials, he extended civil-military cooperation to the repair of facilities destroyed by enemy operations or deteriorated through neglect and to attendance by the Koreans at the local Buddhist temples.[83]

In a study for the Institute for Defense Analyses, H. Wallace Sinaiko adds another example of civil affairs operations conducted in Vietnam:

> A two-man team of Korean medics who knew medical [terminology in] Vietnamese went to work immediately upon entering the country; an observer said that, in addition to the professional advantage of being able to ask simple questions and give instructions to patients, the Koreans were able to establish very effective rap-

> port almost immediately on arriving in a new village. Another medical team – Filipinos who had no language capability in Vietnamese – required an interpreter and, reportedly, were much less effective in their work than the Korean group.[84]

To handle situations in which military personnel interact with civilians, as well as for immediate prisoner interrogation (as distinct from detailed interrogation or psychological operations), Sinaiko recommends the employment of limited-use courses, a concept known to the language-teaching profession as language for special purposes (LSP). In addition to the medical example cited above, Sinaiko portrays naval operations as suitable for LSP: "A Naval consultant, familiar with the nature of the at-sea search routine in Vietnamese waters, has estimated that 50 words or terms would be adequate to handle 95 percent of the situations encountered there."[85] In support of this recommendation, he mentions an instance of a junk that was nearly capsized because its crew could not understand an order to "cast off." Sinaiko asserts that the near-accident would not have occurred had the U.S. crew known enough Vietnamese to give their order in the vernacular.

The differences in concept between counterinsurgency operations and a conventional battlefield manifest themselves in language use also. The military adviser finds himself in a strange environment to which he must adapt his professional knowledge and experience for implementation by a force whose members have radically different cultural backgrounds from his own. (The reader may recall that in World War I, AEF educational programs stressed the similarities in cultural heritage among the British, the French, and the Americans.) Not only must operational concepts be translated to fit the new environment, but the articulation of military expertise must be interpreted for the indigenous commander to implement.

In the last chapter I considered reports by Graham, by Hicks, and by Fiks and McCrary on the use of other languages by military advisers. Although the various authors do not reach the same conclusions as to the necessity for foreign language skills, they all present evidence of greater understanding through higher levels of language competence. Fiks and McCracy alone account for certain important variables. Of their responding sample of officers, 27 percent report they often or very often found themselves with no Americans or English-speaking Vietnamese around; 40 percent occasionally found themselves in such circumstances; 23 percent, a few times; 5 percent, once or twice; and 5 percent not at all. Such isolation could occur in cities and large towns but was two and a half times as likely to occur in the field.[86]

The researchers do account for combat experience as a variable and find (1) those present during combat developed their skill in Vietnamese more than those who were not present when their units found themselves in combat; (2) those not in combat tended to be satisfied with less skill in Vietnamese; and (3) those who were present when their Vietnamese units were engaged in combat were more likely to have used the terms and expressions they listed as most useful than those who were not involved in combat.[87] The authors cautiously conclude that motivational dynamics are such that use of the local language is reinforced under conditions of stress. Adding these findings to the perception of language problems noted by commanders and staff officers in UN commands in Korea, the conclusion is that the more immediate the reliance on an ally, the greater the need to communicate directly. Sinaiko's study of language training for Vietnam finds that the ability to speak and understand Vietnamese "is more essential" at the sector and subsector levels than at higher echelons "because of the lower likelihood that Vietnamese counterparts will speak English."[88]

In the discussions of previous wars I mentioned the magnitude of efforts to translate documents and to interrogate prisoners in order to acquire timely intelligence. Document translation was a sizable task in Vietnam as well. As of Sinaiko's writing (1966), documents were being acquired at the rate of hundreds of thousands of pages per month. Because of the lack of sufficient numbers of Americans with facility in reading Vietnamese, the available information could not be adequately screened to determine the priority for translation. Consequently, enemy operations orders and other enemy plans were often translated too late to be of tactical value. Requirements for verbatim translations can also waste linguist-hours on material that is likely to be discarded by intelligence analysts.[89] If analysts had at least minimal skills, they could determine the utility of documents considered for translation.

Technical and field manuals were among the many items translated from English into Vietnamese. Aside from military intelligence agencies, translations – Vietnamese to English or English to Vietnamese – were produced by the Training Directorate of the Schools Division of Military Assistance Command, Vietnam (MACV), the Joint U.S. Public Affairs Office, the Headquarters Support Activity, and the Joint Publication Research Service (JPRS) of the U.S. Department of Commerce. During fiscal year 1965, JPRS was translating 425 thousand words per month into English.[90] In 1966, the translation backlog at the Training Directorate, MACV, was estimated to be between two and a half and seven years.[91] Typically, the agencies providing the translations were not empowered to reject requests. Consequently there is little surprise in finding enemy operations orders untranslated while FM 12-50, *Marching Band*, FM 35-20, *WAC Physical Training*, and even less utilitarian items are available in Vietnamese.

In the discussion of Korea I noted repeated difficulties in using interpreters. In this regard, the lessons of Korea went unheeded in Vietnam. To paraphrase Santayana, we were doomed to repeat our previous errors. Sinaiko's findings read very much like a dramatic adaptation of a previous work, and, at that, more parallel to a comparison between Lerner and Loewe's *My Fair Lady* and Shaw's *Pygmalion* than between Bernstein's *West Side Story* and Shakespeare's *Romeo and Juliet*.

> The use of native Vietnamese language interpreters has not been a satisfactory solution to the communication problem, although the practice will continue for reasons of expediency. There continues to be a need for skilled American interpreters to serve at high levels in the command and in special intelligence operations.[92]

He notes that the quality of translations is suspect.[93] He reports on "the almost unanimously negative experiences and attitudes toward interpretation that we encountered."[94]

I have mentioned the Asian proclivity for responses meant to please a person of higher social status. Sinaiko, too, finds reports of interpreters who "have deliberately distorted what they say so as to conform to an imagined standard of acceptability."[95] The most flagrant example seems to have been a falsified interpretation during a briefing for a senior U.S. commander. A U.S. interpreter, or perhaps a Vietnamese with many years of exposure to American culture, would not have given false information. (The content of the briefing was later corrected.)

Although U.S. military culture is such that a U.S. military interpreter would not deliberately change the content of a message, even a trusted interpreter is a filter. Indeed, since the message translated must be as consistent with the cultural values inherent in the second language as the original text was with its own cultural connotations, some coloration or slant is likely to creep in that was not intended. Excellent examples are related in the memoirs of Lieutenant General Vernon A. Walters, whose rise to deputy director of the CIA and subsequent appointment as U.S. ambassador to the United Nations were due in great measure to his multilingualism. In a 1959 speech, President Eisenhower paused for Walters's translation immediately after a reference to General Charles de Gaulle as a stubborn man. Not knowing what the next sentence would be, Walters found himself in the dilemma of using a French equivalent that is more pejorative than the English "stubborn" – a choice that might cause the audience concern or embarrassment while waiting for the next translation sequence – or toning down the word. Choosing the latter, he used an equivalent of "tenacious" and set de Gaulle and many others present laughing. The incident made the French newspapers, but, unlike a speech by President Carter in Poland, was well received because of the sensitivity of translation.[96]

The interpreter's familiarity with both cultures often contributes to this linguistic intermediary's filtering of messages. Sometimes – perhaps often – the filter is necessary. The interpreter may wish to protect the image of the principal in much the same way as a presidential press secretary often revises a statement to keep the chief executive out of political hot water. The practice is questionable in both instances, but occurs frequently. Very early in his career, Walters accompanied a group of senior Portuguese officers on a tour of U.S. military installations. In translating a welcoming speech by the commander of the Air Training Command, he omitted a reference to the Portuguese as staunch allies. At the time Portugal was neutral, and the term was inappropriate. Colonel Francisco Craveiro Lopes, who later became president of Portugal, understood the commander's intention anyway, despite the omission in translation.[97]

Walters's first encounter with de Gaulle also turned out to be an incident in which the principal understood more of the original English text than he was expected to. Although de Gaulle had spent four years in England, he was reportedly unable to speak or understand English. Because he would ask for translations of simple phrases, such as a "no" reply by General Mark Clark, for whom Walters was interpreting, Walters believed that de Gaulle really could not understand English. With this confirmation, Walters would add commentaries to his translations for General Clark. At the end of the session, however, de Gaulle took leave of Clark in English and commented to Walters, again in English, on the excellent job he had done.[98]

Walters relates one more embarrassing instance of enhancing a translation. In its move up the Italian peninsula, the Brazilian division apparently left enough of a "signature" for the Germans to locate its headquarters relatively easily and subject it to continuous harassing artillery fire. During a visit to the division, the corps commander made it known he would have no objections to a move of the Brazilian headquarters. Walters, who had not slept well for a week because of the continuous shelling, admits that his translation was more enthusiastically in favor of moving back than the original message. In reply, General Mascarenhas asserted Brazilian pride:

> General Crittenberger, you are an American. You have many headquarters in Italy. You can move them forward, sideways or backwards and no one is going to pay any attention. This is the only Brazilian headquarters in Italy and when I move it, it is going to be forward and not backward.[99]

Duly embarrassed, Walters, then a junior officer, learned a valuable lesson through this on-the-job training. As Walters does not say that either of the principals blamed the interpreter, we assume that he remained the only one who could assess the accuracy of the translation.

The information revolution in which we currently find ourselves has been compared to the industrial revolution because of rapidly increasing capacity for information management. Communication across cultures is also a kind of information management, and the interpreter may serve a function parallel to that of the systems analyst: both facilitate the sorting and transfer of information.

Both also have the capacity for concealing or enhancing information from whoever requested assistance. Walters relates an incident in which General Mark Clark had his jeep pulled over to the side of the road to ask a large group of Italian partisans if they recognized him. Walters, who was Clark's aide, asked the partisans if they recognized the commanding general of the Fifth Army. With the benefit of this clue, they shouted his name, "Generale Clark," and the general was quite pleased. The duplicity in this episode, however innocuous, demonstrates the power of the interpreter. How worrisome when this facilitator works not for us but for the principal with whom we want to talk. And how much the worse when, as in our experience in Korea and Vietnam, the indigenous interpreter often has an education inadequate to handle the material to be translated.

In Vietnam the social status of conference participants was apparently of such significance that the presence of an interpreter – not a principal in the discussion and hence of lower status – could preclude the transmission of information. Lower military rank would compound the problem of status. Sinaiko reports hearsay evidence of Vietnamese officers who would prefer to speak English or French with their U.S. counterparts if there were enlisted personnel present.[100] He also remarks that many conferring principals would refuse to discuss sensitive items with an interpreter present.

The security considerations for using Americans in sensitive occupations with U.S. units, the need for sufficient rank to deal with the principals in negotiations, and the need for adequate military education and experience to comprehend the subject matter that must be transmitted across cultures militates toward providing enough language training for U.S. military personnel to function in another language without an intermediary. Sinaiko's recommendations go so far as to insist that officer linguist billets not be restricted to company grades. Although senior U.S. officers assigned to Saigon could function well in English, it would have been desirable for at least one U.S. colonel representing MACV at the Vietnamese Joint General Staff to have fluency in Vietnamese.[101]

U.S. culture is such that, although Americans may initiate billions of dollars of business contracts over coffee tables, on the golf course or tennis court, or over drinks in a club, we tend to regard the office as the proper sphere for conducting business. By restricting ourselves to office contacts, however, Americans are likely to fail to understand those with whom we interact. Social encounters are therefore not only defensible but necessary in building rapport with an ally. In their study of advisers in Vietnam, Fiks and McCrary write that the percentage of nonduty leisure time spent among Vietnamese was directly related to the length of a U.S. adviser's tour of duty in Vietnam. Although the authors admit that longer tours posed greater possibilities for fraternization, they stress the possibility that the longer an adviser is on the job, the more likely he may be to realize the value of pursuing his task of "building rapport with allies" informally in nonduty situations.[102] Although the authors do not mention whether greater acclimation to the culture led an adviser to extend his tour, the inference seems likely.

Certainly related to the leisure time spent among host-nation personnel is the matter of social invitations. Greater willingness to use the local language probably leads to greater acceptance of the foreigner and thence to an increase in the frequency of social encounters with indigenous groups. Indeed, Fiks and McCrary find "that those individuals who attempted to speak Vietnamese more often were a good deal more likely to receive a greater number of social invitations than would be expected by chance and vice versa."[103]

After Vietnam

My characterization of language problems has focused mainly on events during hostilities, though I have occasionally used a wide-angle lens to capture glimpses of language needs during contingency operations and peacetime advisory and assistance missions. To be sure, the world does not speak English during peacetime either; on the contrary, our need to communicate in other languages continues. Although the documentation of language problems in peacetime is sparse, they have been noted. As part of its review of the career specialty for foreign area officers, the army's Office of the Deputy Chief of Staff for Operations and Plans asked army commands and defense department agencies about their needs for officers with area expertise and professional-level language skills, as well as solid military backgrounds. This review, conducted in 1978, resulted in requests for an increase in personnel allocations of more than 40 percent. Just prior to the review, a U.S. Navy lieutenant with these skills hit the news. As Paul Simon relates the incident:

> In 1977, Navy Lieutenant Howell Conway Zeigler, assigned as a UN military observer in the Middle East, averted a confrontation by speaking to both sides in Hebrew and Arabic. But how few we have encouraged to develop that type of knowledge.[104]

Elsewhere, Simon looks at community relations between U.S. military forces and their hosts. Citing a student thesis, Simon points out that the only Japanese-speaking officials in public affairs at Yokota Air Force Base are Japanese. Local government officials would prefer to deal with Americans, however, because Japanese employees of the U.S. government cannot really be considered representatives of the United States.[105]

My study has shown that the need for language competence may be most acutely felt by the intelligence community, but it is not at all limited to that field. Command and control are impossible without communication. The practice in Korea of subordinating an allied battalion to a U.S. regiment may have been superseded by current doctrine, which seeks to avoid placing a national unit below brigade level under command of another nation's forces – though even here there are exceptions. But the language problems remain. One need only review the after-action reports of recent multinational exercises to discover the continuing need for extensive liaison. CRESTED EAGLE 80, for example, revealed that

> (1) a substantial number of liaison parties for each major staff function are needed but are unavailable;
> (2) a U.S. division is incapable of providing sufficient language-proficient personnel for liaison;
> (3) lengthy delays in planning and operations result from the need for translation;
> (4) face-to-face communication, taken for granted when a language is shared, is difficult between commanders of allied units.[106]

The after-action report asked U.S. Army, Europe, and NATO's Central Army Group to investigate the liaison problem and asked the Department of the Army to consider requiring language proficiency as a qualification for promotion to field-grade rank.[107]

Recently, the Strategic Studies Institute at the U.S. Army War College issued a report on *Non-NATO Contributions to Coalition Warfare.*[108] In the introduction, the authors look at historic motives for participation in coalitions with the United States. Although major factors may have been defense against common enemies, economic and political support from the United States, and influence on postwar peace agreements, cultural and social ties – along with existing treaties and agreements – have also been factors.[109] The authors conclude that closer cooperation among allies and with nonallied friendly nations requires more area trained military personnel.[110] In the authors' assessment, future strategic analyses will require the United States "to view events through the eyes of its allies."[111] To do so, as well as to understand potential U.S. adversaries, we must understand their motivations.

Anticipating the need for continually expanding foreign liaison throughout the decade, the report makes numerous recommendations. Those of most significance for our current inquiry are to advance officer career policies to make the foreign area specialty attractive and to maximize "use of persons with language and area qualifications in positions requiring regular contact with foreign military and civilian officials."[112]

Foreign exchange programs are obviously at least as important to the development of military professionalism as they are to other professional fields. The authors find that the army cannot develop "critical military-to-military relationships" with friendly countries "unless it has personnel familiar with local culture and language."[113] As an appropriate closing note for this chapter, I would pass along the observation that "continued high interest [in foreign area officer programs] could provide important dividends in a major war, but would also help to develop the relationships necessary to deter war."[114]

4

How We Have Met Our Language Needs

> The words of the ambassadors, however, were in an unknown tongue, their letters were written in characters none could read. . . . Silence fell upon the Throne Hall, and the courtiers exchanged glances of consternation. At length the Son of Heaven could no longer contain his anger. His dragon-voice burst forth like the rumble of thunder. "Shame upon you, all you officers of the empire! How does it happen that when a neighboring state sends us envoys, not one among you all has produced a translator conversant with the language and customs of their country? If no one reads this letter within the next three days, your salaries shall be suspended for a year. If it remains unread for six days, you shall be discharged. After nine days, the ministers go to execution. See to it!
>
> –C.G. Soulié, *The Passion of Yang Kwei-fei*

Now that we have looked at our historic needs for competence in minority and foreign languages, let us look at the programs that have been designed to meet these needs. I have mentioned the French classes conducted aboard the troop ships en route to France during World War I and the courses conducted for a fee once the troops arrived. To these programs let us add notice of language study in formal education.

I have noted that the army's own undergraduate institution began teaching languages in 1803, or within a year of its founding. Languages also appear – though inconsistently – in continuing professional education. Files on the curriculum of the Army Command and General Staff College available in the college's library are incomplete, particularly for the period prior to 1930. The training schedule for 1930–1931 shows almost daily instruction in Spanish, while schedules for the preceding and subsequent years give no evidence of language instruction. Records on the curriculum do not explain why Spanish suddenly appeared and just as suddenly disappeared in the following year.[1] Although I have not been able to determine the extent of previous language instruction, holdings in the library of the Army War College show that Leavenworth's military schools had sufficient interest in languages to maintain a department of languages.[2] The sparsity of curricular files from this period, however, does not permit us to estimate the extent of instruction or to list the languages taught.

The Interwar Period

The military services are notable for their historic interest in education. Many observers have long felt that better education opportunities lead to an improved soldiery. Not the least of an army's problems is concern for facilitating the individual soldier's readjustment to civilian life after he has been exposed to the suspension of many of civilization's peacetime values during war. After the 1918 armistice, GHQ, AEF, established a formal system of education to address this latter interest. The opening paragraph of General Orders No. 30 for 1919 reads:

> The Commander in Chief invites the attention of organization commanders and of all officers in the Army Expeditionary Forces to the importance of national education. This citizen army must return to the United States

> prepared to take an active and intelligent part in the future progress of our country. Educational and occupational training should therefore be provided to meet the needs of the members of the A.E.F. in order that they may become better equipped for their future responsibilities.[3]

Subparagraph I–2 of the order suggests offering courses in American and English literature, advanced French, Italian, Spanish, and German. In addition to divisional education centers, GHQ directed the founding of an American Expeditionary Force University at Beaune, Côte d'Or, France, "For the benefit of those students in the American Forces who could not be sent to the French and British Universities and who yet qualified for college or university work."[4] A sizable staff of officers, enlisted men, and civilians offered courses in French, on three levels, and in Greek, Latin, and Spanish, on two levels each. The college of letters also boasted departments of economics, English, history, philosophy, and political science.

The interwar period is commonly characterized as having been an era of isolationism. Language professionals point to a decline in language enrollments as a sign of a national reluctance to project U.S. influence abroad. This argument is not entirely convincing, as the forced reduction in German—enrollments were cut to about 2.5 percent of their prewar level—more than accounts for the entire decline in modern foreign languages. Unlike the decline in language study that followed protests during the late 1960s against prescribed college curricula, the decline during and after World War I was accompanied (and caused) by legislation inimical to the use of languages other than English, and particular hostility was directed toward German. In Nebraska, for example, a teacher was convicted for teaching German privately. (That conviction was upheld by the Nebraska Supreme Court but was overturned by the U.S. Supreme Court in 1923 [see *Meyer v. Nebraska*, 262 U.S. 390]). In Montana, a minister "was nearly lynched for his pacifist views and use of German."[5]

Linguistic discrimination and even flagrant violation of the cherished U.S. principle of freedom of religion were accepted in banning German books and destroying library holdings in German. Such forcible restriction on curricular options notwithstanding, the patterns in high school language courses reflect an awareness of particular cultures that were of growing importance to us. In percentage figures, French enrollments almost doubled between 1915 and 1922 (in absolute numbers, enrollments more than quintupled) and then leveled off by 1934 to a plateau higher than the prewar figure; Spanish enrollments more than quadrupled between 1915 and 1922 and then declined, by 1934, to a level well over double the pre-World War I enrollment percentage.

There are few indications of military interest in languages during the interwar period. Isolated notes on file in the U.S. Army Military History Institute show a voucher for expenses in teaching Japanese in 1920, notes on expenses in language training for GHQ and Army War College officers during fiscal year 1932, and requests for payments for Spanish and Portuguese courses taken through Berlitz in 1940. To be sure, many military and naval attachés learned the languages of the countries to which they were sent, and the intelligence services remained concerned with maintaining a degree of language competence. Naval officers were sent to Japan for a three-year course in Japanese in programs that ran from fiscal year 1921 until shortly before Pearl Harbor. Chinese courses were available in China, and the military services selected officers for training in Russian in programs in Harbin, Manchuria, in Riga, Latvia (a two-year program), and in Shanghai. The British had a Russian program in Tallin, Estonia, which the U.S. Navy decided was unsuitable for its own officers.

Although language skill does not seem to have been widely appreciated during the interwar period, concern for developing this skill was not totally absent. In a paper submitted to the G-2 (intelligence) course at the Army War College, a student in the Class of 1926 wrote:

> Some, if not the best, sources of G-2 information of the enemy are secured from intercepted radio messages, enemy documents and enemy prisoners. To lose or have curtailed these valuable sources of information would be extremely serious and result in loss of efficiency to [U.S. forces] that can only be estimated.[6]

Looking at the anticipated need for interrogators, translators, and interpreters, the student suggests (1) that civilians, if considered as a source of language-skilled personnel, would need time to develop a bilingual military vocabulary; (2) personnel in the diplomatic and consular service and in branches of the government such as the Department of Commerce should be encouraged to accept reserve commissions; (3) businessmen with language and area expertise should be offered reserve commissions; (4) missionaries are likely to be interned or prohibited from communicating and would likely be unavailable for wartime service; and (5) the practice of sending only two students per year to China and two to Japan does not alleviate the shortage of persons with requisite language skills. Using a table prepared by the Military Intelligence Division of the War Department, the student projects that in 15 years the army would probably have 37 officers whose skills in Oriental languages could be put to military use; of these, only 11 would be able to use their language within 60 days; the rest would require refresher instruction to upgrade deteriorated capabilities. The estimate predicted about a third of the officers would need more than six months to recover functional fluency.

World War II: In-House Programs and Cooperation with Academe

The overseas language programs continued into 1941. As U.S.-Japanese relations deteriorated, the location of the Japanese program posed some measure of danger to the Americans. The naval students took precautions to enable them to leave Japan on short notice, and in July 1941, the naval attaché called them back to Tokyo from individual studies and evacuated them to Shanghai. The army's students were not so fortunate and found themselves interned for about six months before being allowed to return to the United States on a Swedish ocean liner.

The military services' own language schools began in October 1941. In that month, 47 U.S. Navy students began programs in Japanese at the University of California, Berkeley and at Harvard University. Later in the same month, the army began acquiring instructors for its own program. On November 1, the Fourth Army Intelligence School opened its Japanese program at the Presidio of San Francisco with 60 enlisted students, 36 of whom would complete the six-month course. With the exception of two Caucasians who had previously studied Japanese, one at the University of California, the other at the University of Washington, all were Nisei with prior schooling in Japanese who had passed personal interviews to determine their knowledge of the language.

After the United States declared war on Japan, the programs mushroomed. The navy found Harvard's program unsatisfactory and abandoned it, concentrating on the development of the course at Berkeley. In June 1942, after the Western Defense Command ordered the evacuation from California of all persons of Japanese ancestry, this program moved to the University of Colorado. In May, the army program had moved to Camp Savage, Minnesota and was redesignated first as the Military Intelligence Service Japanese Intelligence School and then as the Military Intelligence Service Language School.

Both students and instructors were difficult to find. Anticipating its need for Chinese and Japanese linguists, the navy had begun to build a file of persons competent in these languages. Of the 600 in this file in June 1941, half were found to have insufficient skills. Of the remaining half, only 56 eventually were selected for further training.[7] Of the army volunteers, about half had overstated their qualifications.

Some of these were unaware of their lack of competence, as in the case of the major who "claimed he knew Japanese because he bossed Japanese cane cutters on some Hawaiian plantation. He didn't know that the . . . conglomeration of Japanese, English, and Hawaiian spoken on the plantation was not Japanese."[8] According to Captain W. H. Packard's history of naval intelligence, no students of Oriental background were enrolled in the 14-month course at Boulder because it was considered undesirable to have them aboard ship.[9] The army program was afflicted with the same suspicion. The opening paragraph of the "Training History of the Military Intelligence Service Language School" affirms that "Time was so pressing that it was decided to use Nisei . . . even though their loyalty might be questionable."[10] Because of a widespread belief that ethnic Japanese in Burma, the Philippines, and the Hawaiian Islands were engaged in fifth-column activity, the commanding general of the Fourth Army ordered their evacuation from the West Coast, including Japanese who were American citizens—even those who were service members. Every officer and enlisted man assigned to the school was investigated for loyalty:

> Many men and some officers were "blackballed" by the investigators simply because of racial prejudice or because the person being investigated had made a trip to Japan or had belonged to a Japanese athletic club. It is an established fact that numerous men and officers who were declared untrustworthy in the early days of the war later proved to be excellent soldiers and were decorated for service in combat. This problem was finally settled by designating the commandant as the final clearing agency for all students. His residence in Japan plus long contact and dealing with Nisei in the United States made possible the fact that not one student certified by the School was proved disloyal.[11]

The school was to concentrate on refresher training in Japanese for the Nisei and on the acquisition of a military vocabulary. Graduates were to serve as translators, interpreters, and interrogators for field forces. The school was also to train language officers and Caucasian enlisted men to ensure the loyalty of the Nisei sent to the field. Ensuring loyalty was not necessary, but Caucasian language officers were needed to ensure that the translations made by the Nisei were in idiomatic English.[12]

Realizing that the demand for Caucasian Japanese linguists would increase substantially, the War Department established the Army Intensive Japanese Language School by contract with the University of Michigan. Graduates of the one-year Michigan program then proceeded to the six-month MISLS course. Applicants to the Michigan program had demonstrated linguistic ability or had prior exposure to Japanese equivalent to six months of intensive study. Twenty-one instructors in the Michigan program graduated 780 trainees in seven classes. Up to 160 instructors taught at any one time at the MISLS, and during its five-year lifetime, the school employed 328 civilian, officer, and enlisted faculty and produced 5,331 graduates from 7,186 entering students. Graduates served with all three armed forces, with the Office of Strategic Services, and with the Australian, Canadian, Chinese, and Indian armies.

MISLS concentrated on advanced-level skills. There were also numerous other programs that sought to develop lesser levels of proficiency. In chapter 3 I dealt with the purpose of the 10 Civil Affairs Training Schools run by the army and the two run by the navy. The navy schools trained 1,412 military-government specialists and assigned another 201 officers to such duties without training. In September 1942, the School of Military Government estimated the army's civil affairs and military government activities would require at least 6,000 officers, of whom 2,500 would be commissioned direct from civilian life.[13] The Army CATS produced 1,714 officers who would eventually serve in the European Theater as part of a civil affairs contingent of 6,970 persons.[14] The army's Far Eastern program trained 1,570 officers (of whom 220 were from the navy) by October 1945. Recognition of the need for substantially more officers for civil affairs and military government duties led to an expansion as late as the spring of 1945 to train an additional 1,000 officers.[15]

Military intelligence and civil affairs were of course not the only users of language skills. At Arlington Hall, the signal corps had established a course in Japanese that had extremely high entrance criteria. Students had to be college graduates with excellent academic records, preferably Phi Beta Kappa members, with considerable training in languages, preferably in the classics. The signal corps proposed that the Army Specialized Training Division (ASTD) conduct a three-month introductory course in reading and writing Japanese, the graduates of which would proceed to the program at Arlington Hall. The ASTD set minimal criteria of two years of college and a score of 135 on the Army General Classification Test (AGCT). The resulting introductory translation course was conducted at Georgetown and Stanford Universities and at the University of California.

On a broader basis, the Army Specialized Training Program (ASTP) was designed to provide college-trained men for leadership roles in an expanding army. In 1942, personnel planners recognized the need for higher education as a prerequisite for junior leaders. By December 1942, the secretaries of war and of the navy jointly announced the establishment of the ASTP. In March 1943, the commanding general of Army Ground Forces wrote the chief of staff:

> the leaders of combat units, including junior officers and non-commissioned officers of the first three grades, must have a high degree of intelligence and versatility. . . . the basic requirements can be met by the assignment to the arms of appropriate numbers of men who have had college training in the fields of mathematics, physics, electricity, engineering, and languages.

The chief of staff responded in an April 1945 memo:

> The Army has been increasingly handicapped by a shortage of men possessing desirable combinations of intelligence, aptitude, education, and training in such fields

> as medicine, engineering, languages, science, mathematics, and psychology, who are qualified for service as officers of the Army.[16]

Although assignment to leadership positions and to officer and NCO training did not become standard practice for ASTP graduates – a matter of considerable consternation for the participants – the ASTP would rectify these shortcomings across a broad base. Through close coordination between the services and academe, the War Department would set standards, determine the degree of acceleration of studies necessary, and limit instruction to subjects it regarded as essential. In 1943, the army estimated it would need to recruit 199,980 men for the program to meet projected requirements for 1944 and 1945. Demands on the ASTP amounted to 26,758 graduates of the language and area studies curriculum in 1943 and to 16,931 for the first three calendar quarters of 1944.[17] Demands for specific languages or dialects from this program alone range from 12 in Syrian Arabic to about 3,500 in German during just the first quarter of 1943. Specific requirements and enrollments in ASTP language programs in 1943 are shown in table 1.[18] In addition to the requirements in table 1, another source shows requirements for Armenian, Danish, Flemish, Lithuanian, Slovak, and Ukrainian.[19]

Not all these requirements were met by graduates of the program. Battlefield losses necessitated deploying many of the students before they could complete the entire curriculum. Students were not pulled out of their studies because they could be spared, but because the alternative would have been to deactivate 10 divisions, 3 tank battalions, and 26 antiaircraft battalions (and still be 90 thousand men short).[20] Robert Matthew cites an ASTP production report for June 1943 to December 1945 that accounts for 145,068 graduates, of whom 97,812 pursued a basic, nonspecialist course.[21] Of the specialty curricula, various engineering programs accounted for the largest number of graduates. The next largest program was the set of language and area curricula, credited with 16,307 graduates.

A memo from the army chief of staff to the secretary of war and a subsequent War Department directive established a policy of using those trainees separated from the ASTP before graduation as NCOs and highly rated technicians. They were distributed among Army Air Forces, Army Ground Forces, and Army Service Forces (Signal Corps, PMG, and Italian Service Units), and to specific agencies. The latter group, 812 individuals, were individually selected for positions in the Military Intelligence Service, the Office of Strategic Services, and the Civil Affairs Division.

As might be anticipated, the prerequisites for admission to the language programs were relaxed as the war wore on and the manpower pool dwindled. In 1944, applicants for the language and area curriculum needed a minimum of two years of college and a score of 130 on the AGCT. An advanced program was available for those who already possessed considerable language competence and area knowledge. Entry requirements, aside from demonstrated proficiency, included college graduation, a maximum age of 29, and a 130 on the AGCT. (Engineering students needed a 115, and advanced engineering students required an engineering degree and a minimum of 125 on the AGCT). In March 1945, the requirement for previous education was reduced to one year of college; in June, after V-E day, the requirements were further reduced to high school graduation. After the June change, applicants with competence in Japanese were eligible for an advanced curriculum under a new set of criteria: maximum age of 26, high school graduation, and minimum AGCT score of 115. In April 1945, the need for Russian linguists had become so acute that reception stations were instructed to screen for potential Russian interpreters. Requirements did not specify any previous college education but asked for speaking and comprehension facility in Russian (undefined) and a minimum AGCT score of 110.

Numerous language and area curricula existed. Student-faculty ratios ranged from 1 : 20 in programs with greater emphasis on area studies (though even here 60 percent of class time was spent on language) to 1 : 7; the usual ratio seems

TABLE 1
Demand and Enrollment in Area and Language Curricula, Army Specialized Training Program, 1943

	Demands			*Trainees in School*	
Languages	*July*	*September*	*December*	*September*	*December*
Japanese	1,753	1,429	1,044	573	1,277
Chinese	1,123	799	799	406	785
Fukienese	50	50	–	0	0
Mandarin	25	25	–	0	0
Burmese	65	65	50	20	20
Hindustani	37	37	37	17	47
Bengali	25	25	25	0	30
Malay	25	25	–	68	65
Annamese (i.e., Vietnamese)	15	15	–	0	30
Thai	15	15	–	27	27
Korean	30	30	–	30	26
Other Asiatic	461	299	299	0	0
Dutch	119	119	87	0	60
Turkish	218	218	169	138	222

Portuguese	70	70	48	71	71
Norwegian	161	161	161	88	87
Finnish	49	49	49	13	43
Bulgarian	45	45	25	51	50
Romanian	40	40	25	0	0
Swedish	88	88	88	22	20
Hungarian	78	78	63	56	86
Czech	20	20	–	48	48
Serbo-Croatian	30	30	–	75	76
Russian	1,661	1,173	1,173	932	1,192
Greek	67	67	37	71	70
French	1,944	1,586	1,586	1,981	2,029
Spanish	1,221	863	863	1,199	1,230
German	3,493	3,005	2,455	3,298	3,589
Italian	2,292	1,804	1,654	1,552	1,886
Polish	49	49	49	34	34
Other European	741	479	479	0	0
Arabic	92	92	62	158	138
Syrian	12	12	12	0	0
Persian	–	–	–	10	10
Total	16,114	12,862	11,339	10,938	13,248

to have been 1 : 15. In all, 55 colleges and universities ran language and area programs for the ASTP in up to nine languages; most offered programs in three languages. Table 2 lists the participating institutions with the language programs offered by each.

The use of civilian institutions of higher education for teaching languages to service members diminished to almost nil after World War II. The American Council of Learned Societies, which was responsible for the language-instruction methods used in the ASTP, formed a Committee on the Language Program. This committee facilitated the publication of self-study guides in 22 languages. The materials – graded text and two phonograph records – had been produced by the Education Branch of the army's Special Services Division.[22]

Korea and the Short-War Mentality

One of the major U.S. problems with planning for personnel qualifications during the Korean conflict was the general attitude that it would be a short war. From the information I have uncovered thus far, it seems that the Army Language School (ALS) did not gear up for a major expansion, as had occurred to meet the needs for language skills in World War II. Rather, a major effort was undertaken to find a short-term solution to the need.

Instead of sending hundreds of service members to a year-long course at ALS, Armed Forces, Far East (AFFE) established "conversion courses" at its headquarters in Tokyo. Taking military linguists with qualifications in Cantonese, AFFE taught these personnel Mandarin. In the same amount of time – three months – AFFE attempted to teach Korean to personnel with qualifications in Japanese.

The graduates of these programs were received with mixed reactions. Three of the Mandarin linguists, for example, were sent to interpret at the POW camp for Communist Chinese on Cheju-do Island, where they were received with open arms. Despite their youth and consequent immaturity and their

TABLE 2[23]

Institutions with ASTP Language and Area Programs*

Institution									
Amherst College	FR	GM	LA	JT					
Bard College	FR	GM							
Boston College	FR	GM	LA						
Boston University	FR	GM		JT					
University of California									
Berkeley		GM		JT	RU	CM	JA	SC	TH
Los Angeles		GM		JT		CM			
Carleton College	FR	GM							
Carnegie Institute of Technology	FR	GM	LA						
University of Chicago	FR	GM		JT	RU	CM	JA		
University of Cincinnati	FR	GM	LA						
Clark University		GM		JT				GR	
City College of New York	FR	GM	LA	JT	RU				
Cornell University		GM		JT	RU	CM		CX	
University of Denver	FR	GM					JA	BU	HU
Fordham University	FR	GM	LA	JT					
Georgetown University	FR	GM	LA	JT	RU	CM	JA		
Grinnell College		GM	LA	JT					
Hamilton College	FR	GM							
Harvard University		GM			RU	CM	JA		
Haverford College		GM		JT					
University of Idaho	FR	GM			RU				

(*continued*)

TABLE 2[23]
Continued

University of Illinois	FR	GM	LA	JT							
Indiana University		GM			RU	GR	BU	SC	HU	PL	TU
University of Iowa		GM		JT				CX			
Johns Hopkins University	FR	GM		JT							
Kenyon College	FR	GM									
Lafayette College	FR	GM	LA	JT							
Lehigh University	FR	GM									
University of Maryland	FR	GM	LA								
Michigan State College of Agriculture and Applied Sciences	FR	GM	LA	JT							
University of Michigan	FR	GM	LA	JT			JA			PF	
University of Minnesota		GM					JA	FJ	NR	SY	
University of Missouri		GM		JT	RU						
University of Nebraska		GM									
New York University	FR	GM			RU						
University of North Carolina	FR	GM	LA	JT							
Ohio State University	FR	GM	LA								
Oregon State College	FR	GM	LA		RU	CM					
University of Oregon			LA	JT	RU			NR	PQ		
University of Pennsylvania		GM			RU	CM		AD	BN	HN	
University of Pittsburgh	FR				RU			SC	GR		
Pomona College	FR		LA			CM	JA				

Princeton University	FR	GM	LA	JT				AD		TU
Queens College	FR	GM	LA							
Rutgers University	FR	GM	LA	JT						
St. Louis University		GM		JT						
Stanford University	FR	GM	LA	JT	RU	CM	JA	DU	ML	
Syracuse University	FR	GM	LA		RU					
University of Utah		GM		JT			JA			
Vanderbilt University	FR	GM								
University of Washington						CM	JA		KP	
Washington University		GM		JT						
University of Wisconsin		GM	LA	JT	RU			NR	PQ	PL
University of Wyoming	FR	GM	LA							
Yale University				JT	RU	CM	JA	BY	ML	

*Key (Department of Defense abbreviations):

AD=Arabic, dialect unspecified
BN=Bengali
BU=Bulgarian
BY=Burmese
CM=Chinese (Mandarin assumed; Fukienese also taught)
CX=Czech
DU=Dutch
FJ=Finnish
GM=German
GR=Greek
HN=Hindu
HU=Hungarian
JA=Japanese
JT=Italian
KP=Korean
LA=Spanish (Latin American)
ML=Malay
NR=Norwegian
PF=Persian (Farsi assumed)
PL=Polish
PQ=Portuguese (Brazilian assumed)
RU=Russian
SC=Serbo-Croatian
SY=Swedish
TH=Thai
TU=Turkish

lack of fluency, they offered two major pluses: as U.S. citizens, they were considered reliable by the camp command, and because of their own limited education (they were recent high school graduates), they could speak to the prisoners at the appropriate level. The Formosans generally used as interpreters were well educated and often used language beyond the comprehension of the prisoners.[24] Trained U.S. speakers of Korean, who were of Japanese ancestry, were generally not so well received.

In July of 1953, the intelligence division of the UN command was allotted 76 billets for translators and/or interpreters, an allocation considered insufficient by the division chiefs. Command records show that 85 linguists were available for these positions. Forty-six of these were from the Eighth Army (and 10 of these were products of the conversion school) and were generally unsatisfactory. Of the linguists assigned to the Eighth Army's psychological warfare division, none was considered "acceptably proficient."[25] Linguists were so scarce that in the summer of 1953, a redistribution plan was drawn up to allocate personnel resources to military intelligence (including aides to commanding generals, counterintelligence, and negotiations), civil affairs-military government, military police, the POW Command, censorship, public information, psychological warfare, the military advisory group, and troop information and education and to acquire labor. Graduates of the ALS went only to assignments in military intelligence or the Army Security Agency. For the many other assignments requiring language competence, the U.S. command made great use of indigenous personnel who also knew English. As a result of this experience, one colonel in operations in the Eighth Army and AFFE estimated that a future conflict in Asia would require 2,000–5,000 indigenous personnel in addition to U.S. military linguists.[26]

As during World War II, ALS graduates of Asian language programs were typically U.S. citizens of Asian ancestry. This practice does not appear to have been a problem with the Chinese but was cause for concern in Korea. As the graduates of the Japanese-to-Korean conversion courses were frequently Nisei, they were regarded by the Koreans as Japanese rather than as U.S. citizens. The enmity held by Koreans toward Japanese thus had a severe impact on their efficacy.

Language Training Since the 1960s

In the 1960s, interest in language education was pronounced but not solid. The Army and Navy Language Schools were merged in 1963 into the DLI. The DLI became the agency responsible for all language training except that at the service academies. Although the DLI attempted to meet the primary needs for language skills, supplementary programs sprouted as electives at other institutions in the military education system. In a 1968 paper for the Army War College, Colonel Richard W. Swenson reports the availability of elective courses in Vietnamese at the Infantry Officer Advanced Course; in German and Vietnamese at the Signal School; in French, German, Spanish, and Vietnamese at the Armor School; and, using faculty from the University of Kansas, in French, German, and Spanish at the Army Command and General Staff College.[27]

At the DLI, the need for Vietnamese had a curious impact on the curriculum. The course load jumped from 2,800 student-years to 4,800 student-years. These figures would lead us to think in terms of almost doubling students, faculty, and supervisory administrators for the Vietnamese course. But, if a normal basic course takes almost a year to produce a level 1+ in an Asian language, while students may come close to level 1 in about a fourth of that time, it might seem plausible to send four times as many troops through the same facility at a much better benefit per unit cost. In practice, of course, such an approach is a gross oversimplification. In chapter 2, we saw student perceptions of their own capabilities sorted by length of course attended. Although it is true that an individual can expand on the base of knowledge already assimilated with reinforcement and new vocabulary acquired in country, it is also true that the greater the base the greater the degree of progress during a subsequent foreign tour of duty. The question of optimum period of preparation prior to a foreign tour is unresolved and is a current topic of discussion.

Without expanding its staff significantly, the DLI greatly increased the number of service members exposed to Vietnamese. Different resident courses ran 8, 12, 37, and 47 weeks. Vietnamese was taught at both East and West Coast branches and, under contract, at Fort Bliss, Texas. A four-week course was initiated at Fort Bragg, North Carolina. Materials produced at the DLI were used in the contract courses. The contractors providing instructional services need not have been established language schools and were definitely not academic institutions. As badly informed as our foreign policy toward Vietnam is reputed to have been, academic interest in Southeast Asia appears to have been just as ignorant. The MLA, which has been monitoring academic language enrollments for more than 20 years, found that national totals of enrollments in Vietnamese in 1965, 1968, and 1974 amounted to only 20, 19, and 29 respectively. In 1965, only three institutions reported enrollments in Vietnamese; by 1974, despite academic rejection of involvement in the war, the number of institutions teaching Vietnamese had risen to a mere six (Hawaii, Pittsburgh, Harvard, Cornell, and Pennsylvania State Universities and Elmira College).

Language instruction under the Defense Language Program has greatly proliferated since the end of the U.S. involvement in Vietnam. In fiscal year 1981, for example, the DLI graduated 4,412 resident students in 46 languages.[28] Increased demand for resident training has led to severe overcrowding. Until construction of expanded facilities is completed, the DLI will have remote instructional centers at Lackland Air Force Base, Texas, and at the Presidio of San Francisco. Although resident instruction is the DLI's top priority, there seems to be considerable recognition that language-maintenance training is necessary to keep hard-won skills usable. For fiscal year 1981 the nonresident division reported that responses from only half the approved nonresident programs showed language training conducted for 120 thousand students.[29]

The DLI has recognized that numerous needs are as yet unmet. A third generation Defense Language Proficiency Test is being developed that will measure speaking proficiency as well as oral comprehension and reading ability. Separate tests are being designed to evaluate proficiency at lower (0–3) and upper (3–5) levels. Although a shortage of 4,200 linguists has been identified in the reserve components, refresher courses that were most available to the reservists, those at the First and Sixth Army Area Intelligence Schools, have been discontinued. While the army's Training and Doctrine Command, the executive agent for the DLI facility in Monterey, may have recognized the need for an impressive 77 percent increase in staff, progress toward meeting language needs is likely to proceed most smoothly if all interested parties, both in and outside government, cooperate. Mutual support from the defense and academic sectors forms the central topic of the next chapter.

5

Academic-Military Cooperation

> History and language are as important to diplomacy and the defense of our borders as are ambassadors, arms, and engineers
>
> –*Signs of Trouble and Erosion: A Report on Graduate Education in America* (1983)

For military readers whose perceptions of relations between the military and academe are based on their experiences during the Vietnam War, we should point out the level of support provided by academe during World War II. In one of the histories of the ASTP, the author comments: "On the whole, [American educators] are hostile to the War Department. In wartime, their hostility is somewhat tempered, but it is by no means dormant."[1] Such observations notwithstanding, the ASTP was immensely popular with language faculty; scores of articles on experiences with the language and area programs appeared in the professional literature.[2] The cooperation of the language profession is evident in a resolution passed on December 30, 1941 at the annual convention of the MLA:

> The Modern Language Association pledges itself, in this hour of crisis, unreservedly to national service, and places at the disposal of the government whatever special training its members may possess.

The executive secretary of the MLA, Percy W. Long, cites this resolution near the beginning of his review of the association's role in World War II. He then proceeds to recount the breadth and depth of service performed by the membership.[3] In addition to service in combat units and the obvious civilian teaching assignments in the ASTP, members taught at no fewer than 24 overseas locations and served as attachés, liaison personnel, censors, cryptographers in military and naval intelligence, in the Offices of Strategic Services and of War Information, and in producing translations and texts. Long reports that the chief of operations and intelligence, G-2, Military Intelligence Service, the senior political analyst of the Civil Affairs Division, the designer of a 100-volume history of the war (and later Supreme Headquarters, Allied Powers Europe [SHAPE] historian), and the press censor of the British information ministry were all MLA members. (Long also mentions, all too briefly, that some MLA members were interned.) Among the correspondence on which Long based his report are accounts of various contributions made by the language profession. Worthy of mention in the context of this study are comments by several language professionals who relate their use of linguistic and cultural skills:

> The leading linguists in this country were my [army] colleagues, and most of these were members of the MLA .... As a philologist, I was called upon to translate languages I knew well and also to identify and translate those which I barely knew, for their very nature required us to keep them secret from people who would otherwise have translated them easily for us. . . . A large headline in the Washington Times Herald, Friday, Dec. 7, 1945, reads as follows: "MACHINE BROKE JAPANESE CODE . . . " It might be assumed that this has something to do with my story. The said MLA members were also there.
>
> ***
>
> I found myself in a mixed British-American War Office Unit that was almost entirely composed of Ph.D.s in German. . . . Our linguistic training made us prize possessions of our unit. We could, thanks to our research training, penetrate into the innermost secrets of the

> German army setup. Under the guidance of our incredibly brilliant British Colonel, who had been dealing with the Roman army in Great Britain for many years, we . . . built up so detailed an account of the structure and composition of the German army that Admiral Canaris . . . is said to have felt like a lady whose entire past and present had been revealed to the world.
>
> ***
>
> . . . in the summer of 1944 I found myself in command of the briefing house and all of the thousand and one operations connected with getting a secret agent and his equipment to a target in France.
>
> ***
>
> I was responsible for the thirty days of instruction given military attaches, military observers, and all officer, enlisted, and civilian personnel assigned to their offices . . . . At one time there were several sections in French, Spanish, Portuguese, Japanese, German, and Russian, providing instruction at different levels, and a course in Arabic. . . . the O & I Branch had both a broader curriculum in modern languages than any small college of which I know and more students enrolled than a great many small colleges have in such courses.[4]

While I have chronicled here the contribution of the language profession to the prosecution of a general war, both directly in the assignment of military duties to language professionals and indirectly in enabling military students to use more than one language, I would emphasize that these efforts were well recognized. In 1948, for example, an army press release began:

> The importance of training college and university students in the basic fundamentals of foreign languages as a vital requirement for national security in the event this nation is ever forced into another war was stressed today by General Jacob L. Devers, Chief, Army Field Forces. General Devers pointed out that a working knowl-

> edge of foreign languages is essential so that American troops would be able to deal intelligently with the personnel of any foreign allies this country would have in a future war, as well as a foreign foe and in relations with enemy civilian nationals when enemy territory is occupied.[5]

General Devers's remarks were not restricted to students in uniform. A little reflection will lead to the conclusion that the reserve forces and the general citizenry, when called on for national service abroad, should be able to function in a foreign environment. More important, though, is the capacity for an educated citizenry – a sine qua non for a democratic society – to deal with other cultures before the United States becomes involved in armed warfare with other nations. This reasoning underlies the essentially federal interest in developing language capacity in the populace. An honest appraisal of any reliance on academic institutions to meet military language needs, though, has to recognize the shortcomings of current practices in schools and colleges. They simply do not devote sufficient time to developing language skills to make their graduates immediately employable in a position requiring language competence. There are exceptions, and the products of proficiency-based curricula may make this observation obsolete to some degree.

Even without developing competence to a professional level, however, the schools have the opportunity to lay a foundation of skills in language learning in general and in building competence in specific languages. The impact of prior exposure to languages in the U.S. system of education on further training by the military services was noted during the deliberations of the President's Commission on Foreign Language and International Studies. In 1978, the DLI reported that it was having more difficulty teaching its students because fewer of them could draw on previous academic language experience for support in learning a language at DLI.[6]

Both because the extent of language learning in academic settings has an impact on military language training and because academic language learning is in our national security interests, I shall comment briefly on the level of enrollments in various languages. First, however, I shall note an enrollment-related problem, the production of materials to support learning the language.

Two basic factors contribute to shortages, in quantity and quality, of adequate text materials to teach a given language. First, and less likely to be perceived, is a nation's appreciation of a language as a cultural or strategic asset either to be guarded jealously or to be shared openly. Louisiana, for example, recently designated French as a historic cultural resource that deserves special attention to preserve and expand its use among residents of the state. Such efforts and those of quasi-governmental offices that facilitate the use of their country's language abroad – the English Language Teaching Centres of the British Council, the Alliance Française, and the Goethe Institutes, for example – all enable the citizens of a foreign country to understand the culture and motivations of the sponsoring nation. Doubtless, such considerations play a role in decisions such as a national move in German away from Fraktur to Roman type.

On the other hand, a nation may restrict foreign access to its language. In the 1930s, the United States is reputed to have denied visas to German linguists wishing to study American Indian languages. We quite clearly saw the cryptological value of using little-known languages as a secure means of communication. The use of Navajo during the war is a well-known example of a system for easily encrypting and decoding messages.

The Japanese are reported to consider their language particularly difficult for foreigners to learn, and they know that denial of the ability to learn the language will restrict the capacity of non-Japanese to understand the speech and comprehend the writing of Japanese communications. Accordingly, in 1941, the Imperial Japanese government released U.S. Army students interned in Tokyo only after months of negotiation through diplomatic channels, and it placed an embargo on the export of Japanese texts. Fortunately, the U.S.

naval attaché had acquired 50 copies of the Naganuma texts that U.S. officers had been using and shipped them home to be reprinted by the University of California and the Military Intelligence Service Language School. Japanese dictionaries were reproduced by the Government Printing Office, by the presses of Harvard University and of the Universities of California and of Chicago, and by others.[7]

It may be profitable, in comparison with the U.S. experience in Navajo and Japanese, to consider the accessibility of Central Asian languages spoken in the USSR. (I recognize that electronic scramblers have replaced the kind of coding prevalent during World War II, but Navajo "code talkers" were used in both Korea and Vietnam.) A look at the data base on language enrollments compiled by the MLA since 1977 is instructive in this regard. If we look for Kazakh, Tadjik, and Kalmuck (a Mongolian language), and Uighur and Uzbek (two Turkic languages), we find the records reveal that only two of these have been taught in American universities, and one appears in the data base only once (with five students in one institution). Uzbek appears consistently, but with no more than 14 enrollments in a given year. No more than three institutions gave courses in Uzbek at a given time, although seven Title VI centers were capable of teaching Uzbek in 1980.[8] In a report prepared for the Association of American Universities, Richard Lambert and his team of researchers account for 19 enrollments in 1982 (a year not covered by an MLA survey), of which only one was at an advanced level (third year).[9]

A major impediment to the production of texts is the financial disincentive for publishers to issue materials for low-density languages. This problem is now addressed by subsidies available under Title VI of the Higher Education Act (formerly the National Defense Education Act) and through the translation program of the National Endowment for the Humanities. During World War II, of course, the difficulty was probably overcome through direct defense expenditures.

Funding available under Title VI for competitive grant proposals in research and in materials development amounted to $1.1 million in fiscal year 1983, an amount that is about 40 percent less than was available in fiscal year 1970 (figured without adjustment for inflation). This program has not sufficiently stimulated the production of texts. Materials currently available in low-density languages are often inadequate and outdated. Two surveys by the Center for Applied Linguistics show that for Hindi there are 16 texts in print. Half the texts are published abroad, and almost half are at least 15 years old. Of 20 publications used as teaching materials in Urdu, most were produced in the United States, but of those showing date of publication, the newest appeared in 1968 (items dated as recently as 1976 turn out to be reprints of works published a decade or more earlier).[10] Domestic publications tend to be issued through language departments at institutions receiving Title VI funds.

Perhaps it would be useful at this point to define "low-density language." The language profession has grouped its subject into categories of commonly taught and less commonly taught languages. French, German, Italian, Latin, and Spanish constitute the former, everything else the latter. But even among the commonly taught languages, enrollment levels are discouraging. In grades 7–12, French, German, and Spanish account for 95 percent of all courses in modern languages (Spanish for more than half). At any given time, 121 of every thousand high school students are studying Spanish; 67 of every thousand are studying French. Thanks to the suppression mentioned in chapter 3, German runs a poor third, with 21 per thousand, and, in 1982, Russian enrollments slipped to only 0.04 percent of the high school population. Twelve other languages were specified in the 1982 survey, but aside from Latin and Italian none is offered to a significant degree nationally.[11]

Surveys of language enrollments reveal the percentage of students enrolled in languages at a given time. Detailed breakdowns yield additional information to help determine the degree to which the United States is meeting various educational (including national strategic) goals. The National Center for Education Statistics recently estimated that 29.6

percent of high school students take at least one course in Spanish.[12] Such a figure is useful in measuring the attainment of valid educational goals but is less helpful in meeting the pragmatic goal of producing proficient speakers of a language. Until the language profession develops some experience in using the oral proficiency interview to rate students on the federal scale, the capacity of students to use a given language cannot be estimated. In the interim, and for the sake of argument, let us hypothesize that third-year school courses in a commonly taught language produce a useful level of proficiency, perhaps a 2 in the active skills, with many students achieving a 2+ in aural and reading comprehension. (Despite evidence from a 1967 report that this level is attained by college language majors, this level is a suitable goal for all students.[13]) By looking at third-year enrollments, the number of students who develop a useful proficiency in a language can be estimated. The President's Commission on Foreign Language and International Studies estimated that only 5 percent of the students in French, German, and Russian proceed to the third year, thus the proficiency in these languages is probably quite limited.[14]

In the postsecondary institutions, the United States is no better off. Of all language enrollments, only 17 percent are at the third and fourth-year level. In absolute numbers, advanced undergraduate students in French, German, and Spanish number approximately 47,100, 21,000, and 60,300 respectively. The figure in Russian amounts to about 6,600; in Italian, to about 3,600.[15] Enrollment goals set by the Modern Language Association-American Council of Learned Societies Task Force on the Less Commonly Taught Languages use a desirable level of registration in Russian at 100,000 students.[16] Given the current distribution pattern, such a level would yield 23,500 third and fourth-year students, or almost as many advanced students as the United States had in 1980 in all postsecondary Russian courses combined.

The other three widely used languages of immediate concern to U.S. national security – Arabic, Chinese, and Japanese – have made significant gains in the last two decades.

Between 1960 and 1970, enrollments grew by 146 percent, 238 percent, and 279 percent respectively, with additional growth between 1970 and 1980 of 160 percent, 82 percent, and 74 percent respectively.[17] Since 1980, Japanese has increased by an additional 40 percent and Chinese by 16 percent. Still, the numbers are nowhere near the level they should be if the United States is to have the capacity to understand these cultures. For various world regions, there are languages of wide use, such as Hindi (including Hindi-Urdu). In 1983, Hindi (including Hindi-Urdu) was given at only 26 universities (in 1980 it was offered at 34) and Portuguese at only 142 institutions (in 1980 at 149). In a country with 2,371 two and four-year institutions teaching languages, these numbers are small. In their report for the Association of American Universities, Richard Lambert and others looked at enrollment distribution in the less commonly taught languages offered at Title VI area centers. At these centers the need to use the language for research should favor student retention. Indeed, Russian enrollments at the centers amount to 15 percent in third-year courses and 11 percent in fourth-year or higher (compare the national average of 17 percent in third-year or higher courses). Polish, however, had only 2 percent of its enrollment at the third year and 2.5 percent at subsequent levels.[18]

The 1980–1983 figures represent significant growth in the study of less commonly taught languages. In 1960, the MLA's survey of language enrollments tallied 72 languages, language groups, and linguistics (often area-oriented).[19] Although the 1960 survey was directed toward modern languages (current surveys account for all languages), some ancient languages were tallied while others were excluded. The 1965 survey accounted for about 23 thousand enrollments "distributed among some 80 languages, ancient and modern."[20] These were in addition to the top five modern languages and Latin and Greek, which altogether enjoyed 976,511 enrollments.[21] The 1968 survey accounted for 119 languages and the 1983 survey for 129.

The economics of higher education are such that an institution's administration, if run on effective managerial lines, would be inclined to eliminate low-density language courses in favor of more cost-effective language programs. If two faculty members each receive the same salary but the one in French draws five times as many students as the one in Russian, the administration must decide that offering Russian is important to the education of its students if it is to resist the financial pressure to eliminate the program that produces less revenue. Generally, the larger an institution, the more languages it can support, and the more levels of a given language it can support. It is clear from the 1980 survey that the smaller institutions give weaker support to their language programs, as indicated by the likelihood of intermediate course offerings.[22]

If the economics of higher education play such a role in programs in French, German, and Russian, we should expect a greater impact on more exotic languages. In 1983, only one institution reported enrollments in Albanian (10 enrollments) (note one student enrolled in two courses equals two enrollments), two in Burmese (four enrollments), two in Cambodian (three enrollments), and one in Estonian (one enrollment). The campuses offering these courses were the University of North Carolina at Chapel Hill, the University of Hawaii, Cornell University, and Indiana University. Even for institutions as large as these, offering such courses is an ineffective use of resources. External support is necessary. In a useful appendix to *Beyond Growth*, Lambert compares course offerings and enrollments at Title VI centers with the MLA enrollment data (for 1980, the most recent data at the time of his inquiry). Of the last four languages mentioned, three were taught only at Title VI centers, the other (Albanian) only at a non-Title VI institution.[23]

In their investigation of ethnic groups' maintenance of their mother tongue, Joshua Fishman and Vladimir Nahirny note "the eagerness of several smaller, non-prestigeful language groups to endow a chair for their language at various major U.S. universities. It is as much (if not more) a means of endowing 'respect' for the mother tongue as it is of preparing additional scholars or speakers."[24] At best, results are mixed on both counts. Academics, it seems, are not immune to ethnic prejudice, and they have disparagingly referred to such endowed professorships as "rug chairs." Acceptability of the funding for academic programs is a matter of significant concern, and programs have failed to materialize in instances where competing ethnic interests have prevented the conferral of too much respectability on one group. If foreign sources, such as Arab oil revenues, are to be used to fund such a program, concern is usually raised by those that assume this will mean the exercise of undue influence in academe.

Government may also be accused of directing a research agenda or of seeking to attain academic legitimacy for its own allegedly nefarious schemes. In the opening paragraph of this chapter, I cited the historian of the ASTP who remarked on the hostility of U.S. educators toward the War Department. Literature is replete with examples of researchers who sold their souls, as it were, to their government in exchange for support funds. Friedrich Dürrenmatt's *Physicists* commit themselves to a mental institution to atone for the destruction their discoveries facilitated. In Brecht's *Galileo*, the protagonist is guilty of intellectual dishonesty in his self-indulgent recantation before the Inquisition. Defense and foreign area research and policy analysis are all fields vulnerable to attacks on their respectability unless the funding for such programs is rigorously scrutinized by the institution. Funds for language programs through Title VI of the Higher Education Act are acceptable, as the bureaucracy for peer review is unquestioned and the funds are channeled through the Department (formerly Office) of Education. Scholars must be careful when accepting funds from the National Security Agency. Specialists in Africa and Latin America in particular are happy to receive federal funds, but even though their research would be useful to defense agencies, academics conducting research in these areas would not welcome any identification with the intelligence community.

Critics may not recognize that funding for studying a given culture is not tantamount to scholars' allying themselves with any particular foreign government position. Greater support for research on Vietnam, for example, might have resulted in either greater or diminished support for South Vietnam. Without better information on the history and culture of an area, both advocates and critics of an administration's policy argue in ignorance. The federal government is often the only agency with a direct interest in knowing about events in a specific region that is prepared to fund research and language studies.

Despite the tension that exists between campuses and the Pentagon during the best of times and the open hostility evident when national foreign policy is not broadly supported, a working relationship between the two sectors is necessary for each to achieve its goals: for the military to acquire the necessary language competence I have stressed in these pages and for academe to acquire information on other languages and cultures and train others in the use of these languages.

I have mentioned above a growing academic interest in proficiency testing and proficiency-based curricula. In 1978, the Modern Language Association-American Council of Learned Societies Task Forces recommended setting proficiency goals for levels of language instruction. In 1979, the president's commission endorsed this concept "with special attention to speaking proficiency."[25] Also in 1979, the Educational Testing Service (ETS) received a grant from the U.S. Department of Education to pursue a common measure of proficiency that could be applied outside government to the academic environment. The ETS decided a modified form of the scale used by the Interagency Language Roundtable (ILR) was most suitable. Expansion of the lower end of the scale, recommended by the ETS, also features prominently in the provisional proficiency guidelines developed by the American Council on the Teaching of Foreign Languages (ACTFL). More recently, in its adoption of "recommendations to achieve the goal of language competence and cultural awareness for all Americans," the language profession, through the Joint National Committee for Languages, has said in an undated flyer:

> Quality and excellence of language learning should be judged by the level of proficiency attained in speaking, listening, reading and writing on the ACTFL/ETS scale rather than on credit hours, Carnegie units, or number of semesters. There should be prescribed proficiency levels for high school graduation, *college and university entrance and graduation*, graduate and professional standards, and job entry and job promotion.

During the early 1980s, accountability entered the teaching profession in new ways. A spate of reports on the dismal state of teacher education led to new emphasis on competence in the subject matter taught by high school teachers. This concern enjoys a confluence with the development and widespread acceptance of proficiency as an appropriate goal in language education. Application of proficiency standards can perhaps best be seen in a project in Texas, under which students seeking certification as language teachers will have to demonstrate proficiency in the language. Tests, scheduled for adoption in 1986, will include an oral proficiency interview. According to an article by Carl H. Johnson and Bobby W. LaBouve – both of the Texas Department of Education – Georgia and Massachusetts now require oral proficiency of prospective teachers. The article states that California requires level-3 proficiency of teachers who wish to "add a language field" to their teaching certificates, though, if Carroll's 1967 data still hold as a measure of true proficiency, California will not be certifying many language majors as teachers. Connecticut is considering an exit exam to verify proficiency, and Kentucky and West Virginia are considering teaching-field examinations.[26]

At the undergraduate level, proficiency has caught on as the current buzzword for determining entrance or graduation requirements. In the most recent survey of postsecondary entrance and degree requirements, no fewer than 281 campuses reported they had a degree requirement that could be met by demonstrating proficiency in a language.[27] Many of these accept a given score on the College Entrance Examination Board (CEEB) Language Achievement Test as an appropriate measure of proficiency. Two additional campuses accept a CEEB score without calling it a proficiency test. (We note here that some testing experts consider the CEEB an unvalidated proficiency test rather than an achievement test.) A number of institutions state proficiency in terms unacceptable to the advocates of proficiency measures (such as "second-year" proficiency), thus accepting only the terminology, not the distinctions made by proficiency-test developers.

The academic community's acceptance of proficiency standards has been facilitated by eager cooperation between academics and representatives of the DLI, the School of Language Studies of the Foreign Service Institute, and the CIA Language School. Although academics are normally skeptical of cooperation with the intelligence community and the military services in general, the proficiency movement does not seem to have even questioned this continuing cooperation.

Despite mushrooming activity, proficiency-based instruction is not unanimously accepted in academe. In a position paper written for the American Association of Colleges for Teacher Education, David P. Benseler and Elizabeth Buchter Bernhardt point out that only the Universities of Pennsylvania and of South Carolina have an actual proficiency requirement for graduation. (Our tally above is of campuses accepting a proficiency measure, most often as an alternative to the completion of a number of courses). They point out that although the ACTFL provisional guidelines are gaining wide use, they are also being subjected to criticism.[28]

A healthy example of such criticism, which may well lead to greater acceptance of proficiency-based curricula, is found in an article by Sandra Savignon in the *Modern Language Journal.* Savignon's comment, "In its view of language use, the U.S. Government's foreign language rating system is . . . clearly elitist," offers potential for debate beyond the context she sets for it.[29] The remark is clearly disparaging, as she follows it immediately with, "[w]e must ask ourselves if this is the view we wish to adopt for our school programs." The argument demonstrates a dichotomy between advocates of a fluency-focused curriculum and proponents of an accuracy-focused model (not that the two are mutually exclusive).[30]

We note that the ILR rating system is deliberately and rightly elitist, as the model for a language student in any setting – academic, government, or proprietary – is usually the educated native speaker. Drawbacks to the "elitist" norm do exist, however. The speech patterns of expatriate communities, such as those of immigrant populations in the United States, almost invariably suffer under a comparison with this norm, leading to a sense of inferiority on the part of the members of such a community. A current example, visible in the military, is found in the large number of fluent speakers of Spanish who fail to score higher than level 2 on the Defense Language Proficiency Test. Although the norm of educated, native speech patterns is necessary to grade the upper reaches of the scale, these levels are not always appropriate for a given job requirement. I noted in a previous chapter that ALS graduates with no more than a high school background were more effective with Chinese prisoners of war in Korea than were more highly educated Formosans. Similarly, if the United States has a requirement to reach less educated individuals of a given culture, it could adapt the norms of the proficiency indicators accordingly. In such a context, ethnic speakers who are not schooled in their ethnic language may perform quite well.

As Savignon complains,

> Assignment of ratings on the original FSI [Foreign Service Institute] scale was made on the basis of separate, weighted scores assigned to discrete linguistic features. Of all the features evaluated, the *grammar* scale received the heaviest weighting, followed by *vocabulary, comprehension, fluency*, and, finally, *accent*, which had the lowest.[31]

Current distribution of weighted factors at each level is shown in a graph included in Theodore V. Higgs's introduction to *Teaching for Proficiency*. The "Hypothesized Relative Contribution Model," often presented by ILR representatives at the oral-proficiency testing workshops, is an enormously useful depiction of the relative importance of vocabulary, grammar, pronunciation, fluency, and sociolinguistic factors at each level on the ILR scale. The point bears repeating that the scale is normed to level 5, the educated, native speaker. If a task analysis for a given job were to reveal that grammatical sophistication at the 2-to-2+ level were needed, but with fluency greater than shown in the contribution model for this range, we might wish to use a different norm to meet such job requirements. Because of the differences in job requirements, the existing specifications of skill levels for language-designated positions should be reviewed. It is quite conceivable that the existing proficiency measures, oriented to the educated native speaker, do not accurately predict an individual's ability to perform tasks requiring such a revised norm.

Arguments about language behavior for different situations, such as we have illustrated here, are fruitful and are sure to continue if cooperation between academic researchers and government agencies continues.

6

What We Need to Progress

> To subdue the enemy without fighting is the acme of skill. Thus, what is of supreme importance in war is to attack the enemy's strategy. . . . Next best is to disrupt his alliances. . . . The next best is to attack his army.
> –Sun Tzu, *The Art of War* (6th–4th century B.C.)

Since 1978, two major studies have appeared that have addressed national shortcomings in language competence: the report of the Modern Language Association-American Council of Learned Societies Language Task Forces, funded by the Rockefeller Foundation and the National Endowment for the Humanities, and that of the President's Commission on Foreign Language and International Studies. As commissions and boards are wont to do, both made numerous recommendations to alleviate the problems they uncovered. The difficulties they identified and the recommendations that resulted from their deliberations are necessarily general. The pronouncement of the president's commission that "Americans scandalous incompetence in foreign languages . . . explains our dangerously inadequate understanding of world affairs" has drawn the attention of legislators, who have ensured continual monitoring of the federal government's own language needs. Most of these efforts, too, are applied with broad brush strokes. More recently, a Department of Defense-

University Forum has been exploring areas of common interest and means of cooperation. In the report of the Association of American Universities, *Beyond Growth*, more specific recommendations for cooperation are made.[1] Perhaps most promising in any forum discussions regarding languages will be a common interest in promoting student proficiency, identifying more effective teaching approaches, and developing tests to measure competence.

It has been my pleasure in this study to add historical detail to the national discussions. Although it has been clear to some observers all along that language competence is necessary for a strategic understanding of the interrelations of states, there has not been much elucidation of communicative needs at the operational or tactical level. Although I am firmly convinced that world peace depends in large measure on the ability to understand one's neighbors, I hope I have shown that success in war also requires the capacity to understand others. The United States must acknowledge the motivations of its friends to meet mutual needs while deciphering the plans of its foes.

Perhaps the major theme to be taken from this study is that the United States has met its communicative needs in the same manner as it has responded to military preparedness in general: our country has a proclivity for being caught off guard and meeting the resultant demands in a mobilization game of catch-up. Recently, Congressman Leon Panetta was quoted as saying that language competence is as important a weapon as any other. Yet, the military services have given little recognition to either extensive or intensive training to develop and maintain language competence. The following recommendations are made in the spirit of Panetta's statement.

Acquisition of Language and Culture

To facilitate the acquisition of professional competence, army officers should acquire during their undergraduate years at least a level 2 proficiency in the passive skills and a level 1+

in speaking in a language of their choice. (In the long run, as U.S. education improves, these requirements should be raised.) Although my study has not been limited to the army, the preponderance of the information has concerned land forces. Additional research should be undertaken on navy and air force requirements to determine whether their greater reliance on weapon systems rather than personnel justifies a lesser degree of proficiency. Even if an expectation of language proficiency is not instituted for these services, active encouragement is necessary, as bona fide language needs exist that are understated in current personnel documents.

The Department of the Army should consider developing a policy of area orientation, so that career officers would have repeated assignments dealing with a particular area of the world during the advanced stages of their careers. Positions already exist for officers up through the grade of colonel in most areas, to flag rank in some, in which area expertise is required. A lesser degree of expertise, but with a language skill perhaps at level 2, would be useful for most military specialties.

Sufficient numbers of experts in various regions must be available for consultation on political-military matters. Because the need for detailed background knowledge on numerous countries encourages the stockpiling of foreign area officers rather than overloading the existing staff, the services should determine a mix between the active and reserve components.

Interviews with liaison officers from the military services of various nations and studies of the effectiveness of U.S. armed forces in foreign lands have convinced me of the need for familiarization with other cultures. While the inability to communicate across a language barrier is so obvious as to cause us to rush for an interpreter, cultural assumptions about foreigners are far more subtle. To deal effectively with both allies and adversaries, we need to know about their cultural values. Knowing principal motivational factors for a given region is important not only for psychological operations and interrogation of prisoners of war. Cultural familiarity lets us better anticipate our allies' reactions to U.S. policies and procedures and gives us a clue of what they may expect of us. If the United States continues to rely on coalition operations – and unilateral action is becoming ever more unlikely – continuing education for officers must include exposure to the use of interpreters and experience in working with a multinational staff. Current emphasis on the exchange of student officers at various career schools should be continued. Exposure to multinational operations must be extended to more command post and field training exercises and must include the reserve components. Scenarios for exercises must include the activity of civilians in the area of operations as well as provide experience in working with allied forces. When subjected to stress, an allied officer is likely to lose some of his facility in English. We must attempt to meet him part way.

The emphasis on cultural as well as linguistic proficiency that we consider necessary for military operations is probably as valid for other applications of language skill. A person promoting commercial ties between firms or banks needs to know the existing commercial practices in each of the two cultures. A marketing manager needs to know cultural factors that will enhance a product or preclude its success. A diplomat must know the nuances of protocol.

The proposal for expanded cultural familiarity goes beyond knowing not to order Turkish coffee in an Armenian restaurant, not to wrap a gift in white if it is for an Oriental wedding, not to accept a Brazilian's "come over for dinner" as an invitation but merely as an idiomatic greeting, not to proceed immediately to business discussions in some cultures without first asking about a counterpart's family.

Cultural differences may be quite difficult to recognize, particularly in cultures akin to our own. Within linguistic and cultural groupings, cultural distinctions arise that create differing motivations and resultant varieties of behavior. As the anthropologist Ray Birdwhistell noted about the familial behavior of two groups of the Kutenai Indians, who inhabit Montana, Idaho, and British Columbia,

> An Upper and a Lower Kutenai (they spoke the same language) could go to school together, could engage in business relationships and could even marry without ever discovering that they had different views of kinship and family relationships. Insofar as it was possible to determine, when an Upper Kutenai observed an unfamiliar response on the part of a Lower Kutenai, he assigned such variation either to individual difference or to the provincial gaucherie of the Lower Kutenai. The Lower Kutenai rationalized apparent breaches of familial etiquette on the part of the Upper Kutenai in a comparable manner.[2]

Thus it becomes less astonishing that U.S. commanders in Europe frequently hear complaints about their troops disturbing the peace by washing their cars on Sundays. To an American, such a leisure-time activity is entirely appropriate; to a German it is not. And so it becomes clear that linguistic fluency needs to be informed by cultural referents if an individual is to function in another society. Advocates of proficiency measures in various skills have gone so far as to consider adding to the construct of the four linguistic skills – listening comprehension, reading, speaking, and writing – a fifth area: culture.

A recent essay in the *Modern Language Journal* rejects the distinction of culture as a fifth skill, but it is clear from the work done by the ILR that sociolinguistic factors – one suspects sociocultural familiarity – plays an ever greater role as the individual's language skill moves beyond level 3.[3]

If language teaching is to be utilitarian, then, language faculty will have to concern themselves more with developing cultural competence, or they will have to know when to call on social scientists for a contribution to cultural proficiency. It is conceivable that such consultation will need to be extensive. Language is after all a complex artifact of human behavior in a given society. Its ties to political, philosophical, anthropological, and artistic influences are not always recognized. Truly effective acculturation needs to take all these factors into account.

Language Maintenance

The most neglected area in language training is that of skill maintenance. Both from the standpoint of skill attrition and from that of training-funds management, graduates of intensive (and extensive) language programs must be given the opportunity to maintain their competence through refresher courses and recurring tours using these language skills. If career management objectives inhibit recurring assignments, then greater reliance must be placed on the reserve components, where these skills have been reported as being less at odds with individual career goals.

The expectation that an active-duty officer with minimal proficiency in a language can improve his skill in independent study or in voluntary off-duty classes in unrealistic. Group study during duty hours exhibits a degree of command emphasis in maintaining language skills. Refresher courses conducted by, or under the auspices of, the DLI would be among the most desirable options for maintaining proficiency. For part-time, mission-required training to be successful, students must not be pulled back to their units capriciously while refresher training is in progress. Optimally, refresher programs will be integrated with the students' job tasks and teachers will know the job requirements. When such integration is not possible, language-teaching teams need to identify the job tasks their students are called on to perform. For security reasons, many of these teams will need faculty who are service members with a high degree of language proficiency, rather than civilians who are foreign-born speakers of the languages taught.

The length of study necessary to progress from one skill level to the next increases with every level. Although it may take six months of intensive study to progress from level 1 to level 2 in a given language, it may take several years' constant exposure to reach level 4. For the advanced levels, independent study or working assignments with the students immersed in the culture are suitable. For officers with proficiency at or above level 3, therefore, tours of temporary duty in a country where the language is spoken should be encouraged by career managers and arranged in consultation with the DLI.

Language in Reserve

I have shown the use of reserve officers to meet high-level language skills and to deal with the citizens of other countries in their own languages. The principle of stockpiling language skills in reserve was the basis for the 1955 Hoover Commission recommendation that reserve retirement point (now participation point) credit be awarded for the maintenance of language skills. The closest the executive branch has come to accepting this recommendation is the establishment, in 1983, of a National Cryptologic Reserve. Despite acknowledgement of the need for a reserve capacity in language skills, access to materials and the opportunity for both acquisition and maintenance training continue to be discouraged. Language materials are available for purchase but not for government issue to individuals, and the regularly scheduled refresher courses run by and for reservists by the First and Sixth Army Area Intelligence Schools were cancelled in 1983.

Language materials should be issued on the same basis as any other military course and a system of participation-point credit must be developed to reward successful achievement. At the upper skill levels (4 and 5), meaningful counterpart training must be made available on an equal basis with assignments in the service member's branch or specialty. The active agency would benefit from the competence of the reservist, and the individual would maintain both language skill and good standing in a reserve career. With regard to continued use of the language, the perishability of language skills needs to be recognized, and training assignments using these skills must be developed. In much the same way as the West German *Bundeswehr* sends English-speaking officers to U.S. logistics exercises, the U.S. armed forces should send language-proficient officers to function as liaison personnel in bilateral or multinational exercises in which they would use their foreign language skills.

It is inconceivable that a strategic intelligence unit, a psychological operations unit, or a civil affairs unit with an area orientation could fulfill its mission requirements without adequate language skills. Efforts to develop and maintain these skills differ among units and are not monitored through the Defense Foreign Language Program. In 1983, the DLI listed only 36 army and three naval reserve units that conducted language programs approved by the Institute. Twenty-four of these were intelligence units. The remainder have unconventional warfare, psychological warfare, and civil affairs missions. But there are 102 army reserve and army national guard units with special forces, civil affairs, and psychological warfare tasks assigned them (a 1977 tally, excluding intelligence units). How do they meet their language needs? Management information resources should be used to identify all units with language needs, and a central monitoring system should be established to ensure these needs are met.

A 1979 tally accounted for 1,703 FAO positions in the reserve components. FAO designation requires level-3 proficiency, which cannot be reached or maintained without training. Training funds from troop program units and from the Army Reserve Personnel Center must be made available for language training if we are to meet operational readiness goals.

The need for sending U.S. liaison officers to foreign units is recognized during combined military operations in wartime and, somewhat less frequently, after multinational exercises in peacetime. Despite the need, however, organizations do not provide personnel billets for liaison officers. Given the inherent flexibility of the reserve components, the Department of Defense should encourage the continued professional development, both in primary military skills and in language and cultural familiarity, of reservists who could augment troop units and defense agencies as liaison officers with foreign commands and agencies. Such assignments are suitable for mobilization augmentees, who would be available under the president's current "100,000 call-up" authority. Some agencies and commands may wish to fill such personnel billets with two or more individuals per position, so as to have the assets for contingencies in different world areas. This approach to personnel needs is entirely appropriate.

Classification on Mobilization

The United States currently plans to interview its service members when they are mobilized to determine their language skills. Despite the perishability of such skills, the government should identify its language assets before mobilization. Without a language-skill inventory, it cannot estimate current resources, and plans for expansion of language training will be inefficient. Contingency operations, as distinct from mobilization, require the selection of individuals with certain combinations of skills. A first step to identify language resources has just begun. As a result of Operation URGENT FURY in Grenada, the Office of the Chief, Army Reserve, has embarked on a program to identify linguist assets in various military units to ascertain current language capabilities.[4] As automated personnel records become more comprehensive, more complete inventories of reservists' skills can be taken, requirements for proficiency testing can be determined, and resources for refresher training can be allocated.

Expansion of Training During Mobilization

During the last general mobilization in World War II, the United States made extensive use of colleges and universities to meet military needs for language skills. Soldiers became students and were organized in detachments under a commandant. A future global conflagration would not permit the luxury of a year's advance notice to develop programs and build an administrative support structure. Existing regulations require the commandant of the DLI to maintain a list of universities and other nongovernmental institutions that offer appropriate language training. The DLI should not only acquire the bi or triennial surveys of language enrollment conducted by the MLA, but should also consider developing a mobilization-augmentee structure under which qualified reserve officers would be prepared to staff student detachments at various institutions, either on general mobilization or, in the case of greatly expanded needs, in a few languages.

The Department of Defense has in the past lent its influence in the budget-making process of the executive branch on behalf of Title VI of the Higher Education Act. As part of legislative reauthorization of the act, Congress should, in planning for a national emergency, ensure the cooperation of institutions receiving funds under Title VI with federal agencies.

Materials

The DLI has recently been criticized by the GAO for using obsolete materials, even though funds for developing new materials are scare. Both direct funding for development of materials by government agencies (the CIA Language School, the Foreign Service Institute, and the DLI) and indirect funding for materials development by competitive grant awards deserve continued support. Foreign sources remain vulnerable to interdiction, as we have shown in the case of the Japanese embargo in World War II. Domestic production of foreign language texts should be facilitated both because of vulnerability and because U.S. texts can account for the difficulties English-speaking students have in learning a particular language.

Resources for bilingual military terminology available through military publications channels are inadequate. The last German-English military dictionary published by the army was issued during World War II. Although the West German government publishes such a lexicon, it is not produced by experts familiar with the military culture of both countries.

Where possible, such dictionaries should be coproduced by representative combined military staffs with necessary civilian augmentation, so that the terminology used is clearly understood by users of both languages. These dictionaries should also allow for variants in other countries' using the same languages.

Many U.S. military exercises take place using maps of foreign areas in blissful ignorance of the difference between languages. For enhanced realism, exercise controllers should introduce language difficulties, perhaps based on the experiences delineated in these pages. Our allies often send their officers to multilateral exercises to practice their English and to work in a realistic multinational environment. The United States should do no less in its training for coalition operations. Controllers could be active duty or reserve foreign area officers, members of the DLI staff, or officers with experience on combined staffs.

This study of the use of foreign languages by the U.S. armed forces has revealed that language competence is an important component of national defense, both in general warfare and in contingency operations. Traditionally, the intelligence community has accepted the responsibility for developing language skills, and indeed these skills are crucial to intelligence collection and analysis. I have demonstrated that intelligence is not the only military activity affected by language competence. Historical documents clearly show that success or failure of civil-military operations has in the past hinged on the ability to use the local language. Most important, effective command and control require the ability to communicate with allied units.

Minimal language skill takes longer to acquire than most military specialties; professional levels of competence take years to achieve and require considerable care to maintain. To the extent possible, therefore, peacetime training must include realistic exercises and requirements using the languages necessary for a given environment. While military planners must identify mobilization language needs and U.S. forces must develop language skills to a much greater extent, defense agencies must also plan for postmobilization expansion of the training base. Effective resource management requires the inventory of existing language-teaching materials and faculty assets, particularly in the less commonly taught languages. Cooperation between the armed forces and academic institutions would be mutually beneficial: institutions would receive development funds to impart a skill needed for both peace and war and the military would be assured of a base of resources available to meet national foreign policy objectives. Although such cooperation is often difficult to achieve, the current moment is propitious for acting on the agenda of both the military and the academic sector. We should not fail to exploit this opportunity.

Notes

Chapter 1 Notes

1. George S. Blanchard, "Language Interoperability – A Key for Increased Effectiveness in NATO," *Military Review* 58 (1978): 58.

2. Ibid., 59.

3. Speech by Senator Paul Tsongas before the American Council on the Teaching of Foreign Languages, Boston, Mass., November 22, 1980.

4. Kurt E. Müller, "The Military Significance of Language Competence," *Military Review* 61 (1981): 30–41; and "On the Military Significance of Language Competence," *Modern Language Journal* 65 (1981): 361–370.

5. Carl von Clausewitz, *Vom Kriege*, ed. Wolfgang Pickert and Wilhelm Ritter von Schramm (Munich: Rowohlt, 1963), 216. Author's translation.

6. William Riley Parker, *The National Interest and Foreign Languages*, 3rd ed., Department of State Publication 7324 (Washington, D.C.: GPO, 1962), 108.

7. Cited by Parker, p. 107, the story appeared October 4, 1953.

8. Cited by Major Alfonso Troche, "The Foreign Area Officer Program/Reserve Component: A Career Program," typescript, p. 8.

9. General Accounting Office (GAO), *More Competence in Foreign Languages Needed by Federal Personnel Working Overseas* (Washington, D.C.: GPO, 1980), ID-80-31, p. 17. On the other

hand, there were some positions for which the incumbents claimed a lower proficiency level than the one required would be adequate.

10. James R. Ruchti, "The United States Government Requirements for Foreign Languages," *President's Commission on Foreign Language and International Studies: Background Papers and Studies* (Washington, D.C.: GPO, 1979), stock no. 017-080-02070-0, p. 217; or see *ADFL Bulletin* 11, no. 3 (1980).

11. GAO, *More Competence*, 47.

12. Ibid., 48-49.

13. Captains P. C. Marcum and K. V. Montgomery, "Foreign Area Officer Trip Report: *Bundeswehr*," (June 5–July 6, 1978), typescript, p. 87.

14. GAO, *The Need to Improve Foreign Language Training Programs and Assignments for Department of Defense Personnel*, November 24, 1976, ID-76-73. See also *Need to Improve Language Training Programs and Assignments for U.S. Government Personnel*, January 22, 1973, B-176049, and *Improvement Needed in Language Training and Assignment for U.S. Personnel Overseas*, June 16, 1976, ID-76-19.

Chapter 2 Notes

1. Braj B. Kachru, "American English and Other Englishes," in Charles A. Ferguson and Shirley Brice Heath, eds., *Language in the USA* (New York: Cambridge University Press, 1981), 26–28.

2. Parker, *The National Interest and Foreign Languages*, 86.

3. Colonel Conrad S. Babcock, "A study of the G-2 difficulties and disadvantages that May Accrue to Blue in an Orange War as a Consequence of Scarcity of Personnel Familiar with Oriental Languages, and Steps that Should Be Taken in Peace-Time to Minimize These Disadvantages"; Commander D. E. Cummings, "Oriental Language Personnel"; Colonel Will H. Point, "The G-2 Difficulties and Di[s]advantages That May Accrue to Blue in an Orange War, by Reason of the Scarcity of Personnel Familiar with Oriental Languages, *and* the Steps that Should be Taken in Peace-Time to Minimize Blue's Disadvantages"; and Major Alexander Wilson, "The G-2 Difficulties and Disadvantages that May Accrue to Blue in an Orange War as a Consequence of Scarcity of Personnel Familiar with Oriental Languages; and Steps that Should Be Taken in Peace-Time to Minimize These Disadvantages"; Army

War College Individual General Staff Memoranda No. 315 A/44, February 6, 1926. On file in the U.S. Army Military History Institute, Carlisle Barracks, Pennsylvania.

4. Robert John Matthew, *Language and Area Studies in the Armed Services: Their Future Significance*, Report for the Commission on Implications of Armed Services Educational Programs (Washington, D.C.: American Council on Education, 1947). Matthew describes the Navy Language School in his second chapter.

5. GAO, *Need to Improve Language Training Programs and Assignments for U.S. Government Personnel Overseas: Report to the Congress*. Report B-176049 (Washington, D.C.: GAO, 1973), 6.

6. Task Force on Intelligence Activities, Commission on Organization of the Executive Branch of the Government, *Report on Intelligence Activities in the Federal Government* (Washington, D.C.: GPO, 1955), 76.

7. Office of the Deputy Chief of Staff for Personnel, Department of the Army, "Language Training for Officers," Staff Study, typescript 1959, p. 1.

8. Colonel William P. Jones, Jr., *Language Training for the Officer Corps*, (Carlisle Barracks, Pa.: U.S. Army War College [USAWC], 1960), student thesis.

9. House Committee on Foreign Affairs, *Language Training for Foreign Aid Personnel*, 86th Cong., 1st sess. (Washington, D.C.: GPO, 1959), 1–2.

10. Jones, *Language Training for the Officer Corps*, 4.

11. Parker, *The National Interest and Foreign Languages*, 102. Writing in 1959–1960, Jones cites an earlier edition of Parker's work, a classic in the language profession.

12. Jones, *Language Training for the Officer Corps*, 5.

13. Lieutenant Colonel Cyrus R. Shockey, *Language Training for the Officer Corps—An Appraisal* (unclassified) (Carlisle Barracks, Pa.: USAWC, 1960), student thesis. Text secret.

14. Lieutenant Colonel Hanz K. Druener, *The Case for Foreign Language Study* (Carlisle Barracks, Pa.: USAWC, 1968), student thesis, p. 13.

15. Stephen C. Bladey, *Approaches to Foreign Document Translation* (Maxwell Air Force Base, Ala.: U.S. Air War College, 1970), Professional Study No. 4075, p. 17.

16. Lieutenant Colonel Norman C. Watkins, "Cost Effectiveness of Military Language Proficiency," student paper (Carlisle

Barracks, Pa.: USAWC, 1968), on file in the U.S. Army Military History Institute at Carlisle Barracks.

17. See the discussion, in chapter 3, of the use of language officers in Korea. Cf. chapter 2 of Wesley R. Fishel and Alfred H. Hausrath, *Language Problems of the U.S. Army during Hostilities in Korea* (Chevy Chase, Md.: Operations Research Office [ORO], Johns Hopkins University, 1958), originally secret, declassified May 15, 1961.

18. Shockey, *Language Training–An Appraisal*, 44.

19. Lieutenant Colonel William J. Truxal, *A Concept for Language Training* (Carlisle Barracks, Pa.: USAWC, 1963), student thesis.

20. Ibid., 14.

21. Major Katsuji Kobata, "Special Action Force Language Training," typescript N8224.63 (Ft. Leavenworth, Kans.: U.S. Army Command and General Staff College, [hereafter USACGSC] 1966), student paper.

22. Major General W[illiam] R. Peers, "Subversion's Continuing Challenge," *Army* (November 1965), 68–71, 136.

23. Truxal, *A Concept for Language Training*, 21.

24. Ibid., 17.

25. Major Adrian L. DelCamp, "Foreign Language Instruction in Officer Career Schooling," typescript N8224.194 (Ft. Leavenworth, Kans.: USACGSC, 1967), student paper.

26. Infantry Branch, O[fficer] P[ersonnel] D[irectorate], O[ffice of] P[ersonnel] O[perations], D[epartment of the] A[rmy], "Your Infantry Career, Part II," *Infantry: The Professional Magazine for Infantrymen* 54, no. 2 (1964): 8.

27. DelCamp, "Language in Officer Schooling," 7.

28. Telephone conversation with Colonel Edward Thomas, acting head, Modern Language Department, U.S. Military Academy.

29. Reported by Colonel Samuel Stapleton, then-commandant, Defense Language Institute, Foreign Language Center, before the President's Commission on Foreign Language and International Studies, February 23, 1979.

30. Office of the Assistant Secretary of Defense, Manpower, Reserve Affairs, and Logistics, "Foreign Language Training in the Department of Defense: A Report to the Committee on Appropriations, House of Representatives" (March 1979). Testimony in opposition to a foreign language requirement.

31. Study Group for the Review of Education and Training

for Officers, *Review of Education and Training for Officers*, 5 vols. (Washington, D.C.: Department of the Army, 1978). Hereafter RETO.

32. Ibid., Appendix 3 to Annex P, vol. 4, pp. P-3-1 through P-3-11.

33. Office of the Deputy Chief of Staff for Operations and Plans, Department of the Army, *Review of Education and Training for Officers Implementation Plan* (Washington, D.C.: Department of the Army, 1979), 49.

34. RETO, vol. 4, P-3-10.

35. Ken Booth, *Strategy and Ethnocentrism* (New York: Holmes and Meier, 1979), 17–18.

36. Ibid, 28–29.

37. Captain Robert B. Bathurst, "The Patterns of Naval Analysis," *Naval War College Review* (November 1974), 16–27.

38. Booth, *Strategy and Ethnocentrism*, 81.

39. John B. Carroll, John L. D. Clark, Thomas M. Edwards, and Fannie A. Hendrick, *The Foreign Language Attainments of Language Majors in the Senior Year: A Survey Conducted in U.S. Colleges and Universities* (Cambridge, Mass.: Harvard University, Graduate School of Education, 1967).

40. Reading proficiency as the appropriate goal was advocated in Algernon Coleman, *The Teaching of Modern Foreign Languages in the United States: A Report Prepared for the Modern Foreign Language Study* (New York: Macmillan, 1929). Current discussions have progressed through advocacy of reading, listening, speaking, and writing to emphasis on listening and speaking. Some language professionals advocate a fifth skill area of culture.

41. Richard I. Brod, ed., *Language Study for the 1980s: Reports of the MLA-ACLS Language Task Forces* (New York: Modern Language Association, 1980), 11.

42. Barbara F. Freed, "Establishing Proficiency-Based Language Requirements," *ADFL Bulletin* 13, no. 2 (1981): 6–12.

43. For a description, see Albert Valdman, "Testing Communicative Ability at the University Level," *ADFL Bulletin* 13, no. 2 (1981): 1–6, or Valdman and Marvin Moody, "Testing Communicative Ability," *French Review* 52 (1979), 552–561.

44. For a description of the reception of the German *Zertifikat Deutsch als Fremdsprache*, see Ernst Riemschneider, "The Place of the Zertifikat Deutsch als Fremdsprache in the German Cur-

riculum: Report of a Survey," *ADFL Bulletin* 14, no. 1 (1982): 34–38 and Oliver Finley Graves, "The Zertifikat Deutsch als Fremdsprache: An Alabama Experience," *Die Unterrichtspraxis* 13 (1980): 211–216.

45. Lieutenant Colonel Charles R. Wallis, "Maintenance of Advanced Language Skills in the Army Language Program," typescript N8224.246 (Ft. Leavenworth, Kans.: USACGSC, 1967), student paper.

46. Pardee Lowe, Jr., "The U.S. Government's Foreign Language Attrition and Maintenance Experience," in Richard D. Lambert and Barbara F. Freed, eds., *The Loss of Language Skills* (Rowley, Mass.: Newbury House, 1982), 176–190.

47. *Report of the Department of the Army Board to Review Army Officer Schools* (Washington, D.C.: Department of the Army, 1966), vol. 1, Summary and Recommendations, p. 56.

48. Office of the Assistant Secretary of Defense (Manpower), *Officer Education Study* (Washington, D.C.: Department of Defense, 1966), vol. 2, Description, Discussion and Findings, 255.

49. Ibid., 277.

50. Richard D. Lambert, "Setting the Agenda," in Lambert and Freed, *The Loss of Language Skills*, 8.

51. Major Harold J. Hicks, "An Analysis of Foreign Language Training for Officers of the United States Army," typescript 8224.798 (Ft. Leavenworth, Kans.: USACGSC, 1973).

52. W. R. Graham, *A Survey of Military Assistance Advisors* (Alexandria, Va.: Human Resources Research Organization [HumRRO], 1972), draft.

53. Ibid., 142, 144.

54. Alfred I. Fiks and John W. McCrary, *Some Language Aspects of the U.S. Advisory Role in South Vietnam* (Alexandria, Va.: HumRRO, 1963), AD 434 056.

55. Ibid., 7.

56. Graham, *Survey of Advisors*, 146.

57. Fiks and McCrary, *Language Aspects in Vietnam*, 17.

58. Eric Bentley, *Thirty Years of Treason: Excerpts from Hearings before the House Committee on Un-American Activities, 1938–1968* (New York: Viking Press, 1971), 207–220.

59. Druener, *The Case for Foreign Language Study*, 7.

60. Ibid.

61. Fishel and Hausrath, *Language Problems in Korea*, 167.

62. Ibid., 181.

63. C. Darwin Stolzenbach and Henry A. Kissinger, *Civil Affairs in Korea, 1950–1951* (Chevy Chase, Md.: ORO, Johns Hopkins University, 1952), ORO Report T-184, originally secret, declassified 1974.

64. Colonel Wolfred K. White, "Interpreter – or Filter?" (Carlisle Barracks, Pa.: USAWC, 1966), student paper.

65. Paul Simon, *The Tongue-Tied American: Confronting the Foreign Language Crisis* (New York: Continuum, 1980), 46–47.

66. GAO, *Need to Improve Language Training Programs and Assignments for U.S. Government Personnel Overseas*, Report B-176049 (Washington, D.C.: GAO, 1973), especially pp. 38 and 83.

67. GAO, *Improvement Needed in Language Training and Assignments for U.S. Personnel Overseas: Department of State, United States Information Agency*, Report ID-76-19 (Washington, DC: GAO, 1976); *Need to Improve Foreign Language Training Programs and Assignments for Department of Defense Personnel*, Report ID-76-73 (Washington, D.C.: GAO, 1976).

68. GAO, *Improvement Needed*, 1.

69. GAO, *Study of Foreign Language and Related Areas: Federal Support, Administration, Need*, Report ID-78-46 (Washington, D.C.: GAO, 1978).

70. GAO, *More Competence in Foreign Languages Needed by Federal Personnel Working Overseas*, Report ID-80-31 (Washington, D.C.: GAO, 1980).

71. Office of the Deputy Chief of Staff for Personnel, *Army Linguist Personnel Study* (Washington, D.C.: Department of the Army, 1976), vol. 5, pp. 4–14.

72. Personnel Management Development Directorate, United States Army Military Personnel Center, "Survey Estimate of Proficiency Testing and Utilization of Male Officers in Foreign Languages," DAPC-PMP Report No. 58-73-E, Table B, and "Survey Estimate of Proficiency Testing and Utilization of Enlisted Men in Foreign Languages," DAPC-PMP Report No. 57-73-E, Table B.

73. Ruchti, "The US Government Requirements for Foreign Languages," 200–201.

74. Major James R. Holbrook, "Foreign Languages and US Army Officers," typescript, March 9, 1978, p. 1.

75. Admiral Bobby R. Inman, "Language Capability in the Intelligence Community," statement before the House Education and Labor Committee, Subcommittee on Postsecondary Education, typescript, July 15, 1981, p. 7.

76. Major General Richard X. Larkin, testimony before the Subcommittee on Postsecondary Education, House Committee on Education and Labor, typescript, July 15, 1981, pp. 5–6.

Chapter 3 Notes

1. John Adams, *The Works of John Adams, Second President of the United States* (Freeport, N.Y.: Books for Libraries Press, 1969), 47.

2. Captain W. H. Packard, *History of U.S. Naval Intelligence* (Title unclassified) (Washington, D.C.: Department of the Navy, 1978), 2 vols., secret. All references to Packard's work come from unclassified passages.

3. Captain H. C. Cocke, "Brief History of the Office of Naval Intelligence," typescript (microfilm MIC A-14A, Department of the Navy, 1930), 1.29.

4. James G. Harbord, *The American Army in France 1917–1919* (Boston, Mass.: Little, Brown, 1936), 60–61.

5. Ibid., 86–87.

6. James G. Harbord, *Leaves from a War Diary* (New York: Dodd, Mead and Co., 1931), 10.

7. John Erskine, "Report of Progress to July 1, 1918," in Anson Phelps Stokes, ed., *Educational Plans for the American Army Abroad* (New York: Association Press, 1918), 58; "Report on Condition of the Work, October 1, 1918," in Stokes, p. 81.

8. Stokes, *Educational Plans*, "Educational Memorandum No. 1."

9. On the training and use of U.S. units with the British and French, see Historical Division, Department of the Army, *United States Army in the World War, 1917-1919*, vol. 3 (Washington, D.C.: GPO, 1948).

10. See Dorothy Waggoner, "Statistics on Language Use," in Charles A. Ferguson and Shirley Brice Heath, eds., *Language in the USA* (New York: Cambridge University Press, 1981), 486–515.

11. General Headquarters, American Expeditionary Force, "Provisional Intelligence Manual, A.E.F." (Washington, D.C.: Office of the Chief of Staff, War Department, 1918), mimeographed typescript, originally classified confidential, declassified 1949, pp. 2, 34.

12. Military Intelligence Division, General Staff, *Provisional*

Combat Intelligence Manual (Washington, D.C.: War Department, 1918), originally classified confidential, declassified 1949, pp. 8–9. We would add that interrogation was begun at the regimental level but was primarily a function of the corps intelligence section, according to *Regulations for the Intelligence Section of the General Staff* (Paris: Headquarters, AEF, 1917), originally classified secret, declassified 1949, pp. 22–23.

13. "General Staff College, Langres, 1918, G–Z," bound, mimeographed notes, lecture no. 7, second course, p. 2. Nonmilitary readers please note that "order of battle" refers to the organization, rank, structure, uniforms, and identification of personnel of an armed force, either friendly or hostile. Although not mentioned in the lecture notes, there was also an intelligence section at the battalion level.

14. General Headquarters, AEF, "Provisional Intelligence Manual, A.E.F." (corporate author and title are identified in pencil), mimeographed typescript, (Washington, D.C.: Office of the Chief of Staff, War Department, 1918), 18–19.

15. Packard, *History of U.S. Naval Intelligence*, 2g4, 2g5.

16. Ibid., 2g5.

17. Ibid., 2g4, 2g6.

18. Mario A. Pei, *Languages for War and Peace*, 2nd ed. (New York: Vanni, 1945), 11.

19. Curricula Branch, Army School Division, Army Service Forces, "A History of the Army Specialized Training Program from its Beginning to December 1944. Supplement to 30 June 1945" (Washington, D.C.: Office of the Chief of Military History [OCMH], 1945), typescript 3–4.1A/AA, vol. 2, originally secret, declassified October 1945, pp. 3–4.

20. Major Richard Riccardelli, "Electronic Warfare in WW II," *Army Communicator* (Winter 1985), 43.

21. Letter, Eisenhower to Marshall, November 30, 1942, cited in Harry L. Coles and Albert K. Weinberg, *Civil Affairs: Soldiers Become Governors*, United States Army in World War II, Special Studies (Washington, D.C.: OCMH, 1964), 3; cited again, 45.

22. Ibid., 4.

23. Letter, Harold Ickes, secretary of the interior, to President Roosevelt, December 28, 1942, cited by Coles and Weinberg, *Civil Affairs*, 25.

24. Special Staff, U.S. Army, "History of Training – Military

Government" (Washington, D.C.: OCMH, n.d.), vol. 1, 1939–1944, OCMH typescript 4-4/CE, originally secret, now unclassified, p. 10. Hereafter cited as "Military Government."

25. Saul K. Padover, memo for Secretary Ickes, January 8, 1943, cited by Coles and Weinberg, *Civil Affairs*, 26. Padover, a historian, was an assistant to Ickes from 1938 to 1943. Elsewhere in his memo, he laments the militarization of social scientists, administrators, "scientific" managers, lawyers, and others. Padover's fear that the military was monopolizing the pool of skilled labor was to take an ironic twist, as he accepted a commission as a lieutenant colonel.

26. Franklin D. Roosevelt, memo to the secretary of war, October 29, 1942, cited in Coles and Weinberg, *Civil Affairs*, 22.

27. "Military Government," 1.

28. Ibid., 5.

29. Ibid., 4.

30. Ibid., 3.

31. Provost Marshal General's Office, "History of Military Government Training" (Washington, D.C.: OCMH, 1946), typescript 4-4/DA, p. 1. This typescript and the one cited in note 24 are quite similar; they duplicate passages verbatim but are not identical. The researcher should also note that some of these typescripts differ between hard copy and microfilm copy.

32. Ibid., 84.

33. Ibid., 13–14.

34. Ibid., 72.

35. Ibid., 44.

36. "History of the Civil Affairs Training School at Yale University," in "History of Military Government Training" (Washington, D.C.: OCMH, 1945), typescript 4-4.4A/AA, p. 3.

37. Major Robert C. McCaleb, "Revision of Eighth US Army Linguist and Rotation Policy," Eighth Army Staff Memorandum, June 28, 1953, cited by Fishel and Hausrath, *Language Problems in Korea*; Office of the Chief, Army Field Forces, Department of the Army, AFFE (Armed Forces, Far East) Observer Team No. 5 Report, July 1951; Team No. 6 Report, March 1952; Team No. 7 Report, November 1952; Team No. 8 Report, May 1953; Observer Team Reports are cited by Fishel and Hausrath.

38. Fishel and Hausrath, *Language Problems in Korea*, 13.

39. Ibid., 17.
40. Ibid., 15.
41. Ibid., 18.
42. Ibid., 22.
43. Ibid., 62.
44. Ibid., 62–63.

45. Colonel Wallace W. Wilkins, Jr., "You Are What You Say" (Carlisle Barracks, Pa.: USAWC, 1967) student paper, 9.

46. Major William J. Fox, *Inter-Allied Co-operation during Combat Operations*, History of the Korean War, vol. 3 (Washington, D.C.: OCMH, n.d.). On microfilm (reel A141), the typescript is considered vol. 1. Originally secret, the volume was declassified in 1975.

47. Captain Richard L. Harwell, U.S. signal adviser to the Turkish Armed Forces Command, letter to signal officer, 25th Infantry Division, subject: Problems encountered in working with UN forces, October 28, 1951, cited by Fox, *Inter-Allied Co-operation*, who received the information indirectly from Colonel Richard W. Whitney, chief of staff of the division. This letter and subsequent ones cited are all to be found in the annex to Fox's narrative. As these letters are numbered by hand in the typescript, as well as numbered in the original, I have opted here to cite letters directly with their original pagination.

48. See Fox, *Inter-Allied Co-operation*, 88.

49. Colonel W. C. Bullock, commander, Second Division Artillery, letter to Major Fox dated November 28, 1951.

50. Druener, *The Case for Foreign Language Study*, 6.

51. Colonel Kebbede Guebre, commanding officer, Ethiopian Expeditionary Forces in Korea, letter to General Headquarters, Eighth U.S. Army, Korea, dated January 1, 1952, p. 3.

52. Major Ray S. Sibert, adjutant, 21st U.S. Infantry Regiment, letter to chief of staff, 24th Infantry Division, subject: Questionnaire on coordination and utilization of UN units, dated November 28, 1951.

53. Logistic support was not a "national responsibility" during the Korean War. Extensive support was provided UN units by the United States.

54. Brigadier General Thomas L. Harrold, deputy commander, First U.S. Corps, letter to Major Fox dated December 15, 1951, p. 2.

55. Colonel W. A. Harris, commander, 7th U.S. Cavalry

Regiment, letter to Major Fox, in Fox, *Inter-Allied Co-operation*, n.d., Annex, 106.

56. Colonel W. C. Bullock, in Fox, *Inter-Allied Co-operation*.

57. Stolzenbach and Kissinger, *Civil Affairs in Korea, 1950–51*.

58. Ibid., 168.

59. Fishel and Hausrath, *Language Problems in Korea*, 167.

60. Ibid., 168.

61. Ibid., 169.

62. Ibid., 173.

63. Ibid., 174.

64. Ibid., 183.

65. Ibid.

66. Ibid., 191.

67. Ibid., 201.

68. John F. Kennedy, memorandum for the secretary of defense, February 16, 1963. Copy on file among the papers of Brigadier General Henry C. Newton, U.S. Army Military History Institute, Carlisle Barracks, Pa.

69. Simon, in *The Tongue-Tied American*, notes that the Foreign Service Institute was established during the beginning of George C. Marshall's tenure as secretary of state, p. 146.

70. Gerald C. Bailey, *The Utilization of Foreign Languages in Naval Psychological Operations* (McLean, Va.: Human Sciences Research, Inc., 1964), Report HSR-RR-66/9As, p. 25.

71. Howard C. Reese, *Area Handbook for Tunisia* (Washington, D.C.: GPO, 1970), 66.

72. Jesse Levitt, "French as a World Language," *Geolinguistics* 5 (1979): 62. Levitt cites as his source a newspaper article by Henry Giniger, "Some Arabs Stay in the French Orbit," *New York Times*, March 11, 1973, part 1, p. 17.

73. Letter, Major General T. J. Conway to Brigadier General Henry C. Newton, February 18, 1963, p. 1; on file among the Henry C. Newton papers, U.S. Army Military History Institute, Carlisle Barracks, Pa.

74. Bailey, *Utilization*, 26.

75. Ibid., 26.

76. Ibid., 29.

77. Ibid.

78. Commander John F. Sullivan, USN, *The Language Weapon: Usefulness and Readiness* (Carlisle Barracks, Pa.: USAWC,

1966), student thesis, 9.

79. Lieutenant General Stanley Robert Larsen and Brigadier General James Lawton Collins, Jr., *Allied Participation in Vietnam* (Washington, D.C.: Department of the Army, 1975), table 1, p. 23.

80. Ibid., 19.

81. Ibid., 143.

82. Ibid., 145.

83. Ibid., 135.

84. H. Wallace Sinaiko, *Foreign Language Training: An Investigation of Research and Development for Vietnam* (Arlington, Va.: Institute for Defense Analyses, 1966), Study S-232, AD 632 916, p. 46.

85. Ibid., 46.

86. Fiks and McCrary, *Some Language Aspects of the U.S. Advisory Role in South Vietnam*, 8.

87. Ibid., 13.

88. Fiks and McCrary, *Language Aspects in Vietnam*, 12.

89. Bladey, *Document Translation*, 4.

90. Sinaiko, *Research and Development for Vietnam*, 64.

91. Ibid., 61.

92. Ibid., 4.

93. Ibid., 5.

94. Ibid., 23–24.

95. Ibid., 24.

96. Vernon A. Walters, *Silent Missions* (Garden City, N.Y.: Doubleday, 1978), 495.

97. Ibid., 63.

98. Ibid., 98–99.

99. Ibid., 133.

100. Sinaiko, *Research and Development for Vietnam*, 24–25.

101. Ibid., 13.

102. Fiks and McCrary, *Language Aspects in Vietnam*, 13.

103. Ibid., 14.

104. Simon, *The Tongue-Tied American*, 7.

105. For his discussion, see Simon, *The Tongue-Tied American*, 52–53. Simon cites Elizabeth Lubin, "American Military and Japanese Municipality at the Interface of Culture: Official Relations Between U.S. Bases and Local Communities in Japan," unpublished thesis, Harvard University, 1979, especially pp. 55–62.

106. U.S. Army, Europe, and Seventh Army, "Exercise Crested

Eagle 80: Lessons Learned," unclassified (Heidelberg: U.S. Army, Europe, and Seventh Army, 1980), bound typescript, secret, 46–47. Findings cited are unclassified.

107. Ibid., p. 47.

108. Strategic Studies Institute, USAWC, *Non-NATO Contributions to Coalition Warfare*, vol. 1, Basic Report, unclassified (Carlisle Barracks, Pa.: USAWC, 1981).

109. Ibid., vii.

110. Ibid., x.

111. Ibid., 10.

112. Ibid., 37.

113. Ibid., 29.

114. Ibid.

Chapter 4 Notes

1. *Schedule for 1930–1931, First Year Course, The Command and General Staff School* (Ft. Leavenworth, Kans.: Command and General Staff School Press, 1930).

2. Though not among the library holdings of the institution that produced it, the following book is available in the library of the USAWC, at Carlisle Barracks, Pa. Department of Languages, The Army Service Schools, *Language Notes and A Brief History of the English, French, German and Spanish Languages* (Ft. Leavenworth, Kans.: Army Service Schools Press, 1917).

3. General Headquarters, AEF, General Orders No. 30, France, February 13, 1919.

4. Headquarters, American Expeditionary Force University, *The Catalogue*, Bulletin 91, Part 1 (Beaune, France: American Expeditionary Force University, 1919), 4.

5. Anthony F. Beltramo, "Profile of a State: Montana," in Ferguson and Heath, *Language in the USA*, 35.

6. Individual General Staff Memoranda, *A Study of the G-2 Difficulties and Disadvantages that May Accrue to Blue in an Orange War as a Consequence of Scarcity of Personnel Familiar with Oriental Languages; and the Steps that Should be Taken in Peace-time to Minimize these Disadvantages* (Washington Barracks, D.C.: The Army War College, 1926). Student papers on file in the U.S. Army Military History Institute, Carlisle Barracks, Pa.

7. Robert John Matthew, *Language and Area Studies in the Armed Services* (Washington, D.C.: American Council on Education, 1947), 15.

8. Intelligence Division, War Department General Staff, "Training History of the Military Intelligence Service Language School," (Washington, D.C.: Office of the Chief of Military History [OCMH], [1949]), typescript 2-2.2B/AA, vol. 2, p. 2. Hereafter cited as MISLS 2; vol. 1 cited as MISLS 1.

9. Captain W. H. Packard, *History of U.S. Naval Intelligence* (Title unclassified) (Washington, D.C.: Department of the Navy, 1978), 2 vols., secret, 8, 9. All references from Packard's work are taken from unclassified passages.

10. MISLS 1, p. 4.

11. MISLS 1, p. 5. According to MISLS 1, the evacuation order was promulgated by the Fourth Army. Packard, *History of U.S. Naval Intelligence*, p. 8.8, claims it was given by the Western Defense Command.

12. MISLS 1, pp. 6–7.

13. Provost Marshal General's Office, "History of Military Government Training" (Washington, D.C.: OCMH, 1945), typescript 4-4/DA, vol. 1, pp. 11–12. Originally secret, declassified 1945.

14. Ibid., vol. 4, p. 110.

15. Provost Marshal General's Office, "History of Military Government Training covering the Period 1 July to 31 December 1945" (Washington, D.C.: OCMH, 1945), typescript 4-4/DB p. 2. Originally secret, declassified 1945. Researchers should note that documents from this era exist in multiple versions in hard copy and on microfilm. The various editions often do not coincide in authorship, title, pagination, volume designations, security classifications, and dates of publication. These differences occur even where the various versions carry the same catalog number.

16. Curriculum Branch, School Division, Army Service Forces, "A History of the Army Specialized Training Program from its Beginning to 31 December 1944" (Washington, D.C.: OCMH, 1944), typescript 3–4.1A/AA, vol. 1, p. 6. Originally confidential, declassified October 1945.

17. Chart, "Summary of ASTP Demands, January 1943–July 1944," in Curricula Branch, School Division, Army School Division, Army Service Forces, "A History of the Army Specialized Training Program from its Beginning to 31 December 1944" (Washing-

ton, D.C.: OCMH, 1945), typescript 3–4.1A/AA, following p. 30, originally classified secret, declassified 1945.

18. Chart, "Fluctuation of Foreign Area and Language Demands," in "A History of the Army Specialized Training Program," (footnote no. 16) following p. 30.

19. Curriculum Branch, School Division, Army Service Forces, "History of Military Training, Army Specialized Training Program, from its Beginning to 31 December 1944, with supplement to 30 June 1945," (Washington, D.C.: OCMH, 1945), typescript 3–4.1A/AA, vol. 1. Originally classified confidential, declassified 1945. See chart VI, following p. 47.

20. Memo for the Secretary of War from the Chief of Staff of the Army, Subject: Serious Personnel Shortages, 10 February 1944, cited in typescript 3–4.1A/AA, pp. 168–170 (hand-numbered pages).

21. Matthew, *Language and Area Studies in the Armed Services*, 187.

22. Judith E. Liskin-Gasparro, "The ACTFL Proficiency Guidelines: A Historical Perspective," in Theodore V. Higgs, ed., *Teaching for Proficiency, the Organizing Principle* (Lincolnwood, Ill.: National Textbook Co., 1984), ACTFL Foreign Language Education Series, p. 18.

23. Ibid., p. 25. Robert J. Matthew, *Language and Area Studies in the Armed Services*, Appendix A, pp. 177–178. Matthew does not account for dialects, e.g., Fukienese (Chinese) and Syrian (Arabic), or for requirements identified in table 1 as "other Asiatic" and "other European." Available sources do not confirm whether these needs were ever met.

24. Fishel and Hausrath, *Language Problems of the US Army During Hostilities in Korea*, 200–201.

25. Ibid., 57, 58.

26. Ibid., 61.

27. Colonel Richard W. Swenson, "So You Want to Communicate? The Case for Foreign Language," student paper (USAWC, 1968), on file in the U.S. Army Military History Institute, Carlisle Barracks, Pa., 12.

28. Defense Language Institute, Foreign Language Center, *Annual Program Review*, February 10–12, 1982 (Presidio of Monterey, California: Defense Language Institute, 1982), 5.

29. Ibid., 26.

Chapter 5 Notes

1. Curricula Branch, "A History of the Army Specialized Training Program from its Beginning to 31 December 1944," p. 62. (See chapter 4, footnote no. 17.)

2. For a list, see the bibliography to Matthew, *Language and Area Studies in the Armed Services.*

3. Percy W. Long, "The Modern Language Association of America in World War II," *PMLA: Proceedings* 64 (1948): 45–78.

4. Ibid., 66–68, 70.

5. Cited in Parker, *The National Interest and Foreign Languages*, 104.

6. "Suggested Topics for Discussion by the President's Commission on Foreign Language and International Studies from the Defense Language Institute Foreign Language Center," typescript (1978), 3.

7. Intelligence Division, War Department General Staff, "Training History of the Military Intelligence Service Language School" (Washington, D.C.: OCMH, [1949]), typescript 2-2.B/AA, vol. 1, p. 28. This source contains no discussion of copyright or royalty issues.

8. Telephone conversation with Dr. Richard T. Thompson, Center for International Education, U.S. Department of Education, August 13, 1985.

9. Interpolated from two charts in Appendix E of Richard D. Lambert et al., *Beyond Growth: The Next Stage in Language and Area Studies* (Washington, D.C.: Association of American Universities [AAU], 1984), 321, 323.

10. Dora E. Johnson et al., eds., *A Survey of Materials for the Study of the Uncommonly Taught Languages: South Asia*, vol. 4, (Arlington, Va.: Center for Applied Linguistics, 1976). Deborah H. Hatfield, et al., eds., *A Survey of Materials for the Study of the Uncommonly Taught Languages: Supplement 1976–81*, ED 228 863.

11. American Council on the Teaching of Foreign Languages, "Foreign Language Enrollments in Public Secondary Schools, Fall 1982," *Foreign Language Annals* 17 (1984): 611–623.

12. William B. Fetters and Jeffrey A. Owings, "High School and Beyond: Tabulation – Foreign Language Courses Taking by 1980 High School Sophomores who Graduated in 1982." (Washington, D.C.: National Center for Education Statistics, 1984), type-

script LSB 84-4-16.

13. John B. Carroll et al., *The Foreign Language Attainments of Foreign Language Majors in the Senior Year.*

14. President's Commission on Foreign Language and International Studies, *Strength through Wisdom: A Critique of U.S. Capability* (Washington, D.C.: GPO, 1979), 9.

15. For a detailed description of postsecondary language enrollments, by level, see Kurt E. Müller, "The Distribution of Language Enrollments in Two- and Four-Year Institutions of Higher Education in the United States," *ADFL Bulletin* 13, no. 2 (1982): 5–12. Estimates given here are calculated by the percentage of advanced enrollments reported for 1980 – the only distribution sampling ever undertaken by the Modern Language Association (MLA). For 1983 enrollment information, see Richard I. Brod and Monica S. Devens, "Foreign Language Enrollments in U.S. Institutions of Higher Education – Fall 1983," *ADFL Bulletin* 16, no. 2 (1985): 57–63.

16. Leon I. Twarog, "A National Ten-Year Plan for Teaching and Training in the Less Commonly Taught Languages: Source Materials for the Report of the Task Force on the Less Commonly Taught Languages," in Richard I. Brod, ed., *Language Study for the 1980s*, 38–77.

17. Kurt E. Müller, "Foreign Language Enrollments in U.S. Institutions of Higher Education – Fall 1980," *ADFL Bulletin* 13, no. 2 (1981): 31–36.

18. See Richard D. Lambert et al., *Beyond Growth*, appendix E, pp. 319–324.

19. Mara Vamos, John Harmon, Hannelore Fischer-Lorenz, and Frank White, "Modern Foreign Language Enrollments in Four-Year Colleges and Universities, Fall 1960," in MLA, *Reports of Surveys and Studies in the Teaching of Modern Foreign Languages* (New York: MLA, 1961), 125.

20. Nina Greer Herslow and James F. Dersham, *Foreign Language Enrollments in Institutions of Higher Education, Fall 1965* (New York: MLA), vii.

21. Ibid., iv–vi.

22. Kurt E. Müller, "The Distribution of Language Enrollments," 9, table 4.

23. Lambert et al., *Beyond Growth*, Appendix D, 306–318.

24. Joshua A. Fishman and Vladimir C. Nahirny, "The Ethnic Group School and Mother Tongue Maintenance," in Fishman, et al., eds., *Language Loyalty in the United States: The Maintenance*

and Perpetuation of Non-English Mother Tongues by American Ethnic and Religious Groups (The Hague: Mouton, 1966), 123.

25. President's Commission on Foreign Language and International Studies, *Strength through Wisdom*, 38.

26. Carl H. Johnson and Bobby W. LaBouve, "A Status Report on the Testing of Prospective Language Teachers for Initial State Certification," *Foreign Language Annals* 17 (1984): 461–472, especially pp. 462–467.

27. Richard I. Brod and Carl R. Lovitt, "The MLA Survey of Foreign Language Entrance and Degree Requirements," *ADFL Bulletin* 15, no. 3 (1984): 46–58.

28. David P. Benseler and Elizabeth Buchter Bernhardt, "Foreign Languages and Global Studies: A Position Paper," typescript (Columbus, Ohio: Ohio State University, 1985), 10–11. Position paper written for the American Association of Colleges for Teacher Education.

29. Sandra J. Savignon, "Evaluation of Communicative Competence: The ACTFL Provisional Proficiency Guidelines," *Modern Language Journal* 69 (1985): 132.

30. For my part, I side with those who insist that students actively use the language being learned and receive sufficient correction to avoid "error fossilization." See, for example, Theodore V. Higgs, ed., *Teaching for Proficiency, the Organizing Principle* (Lincolnwood, Ill.: National Textbook Co., 1984); John F. Lalande II, "An Error in Error-Correction Policies?" *ADFL Bulletin* 12, no. 3 (1981): 45–47.

31. Savignon, "Evaluation of Communicative Competence," 131.

Chapter 6 Notes

1. Richard D. Lambert et al., *Beyond Growth*, 257–281.

2. Ray L. Birdwhistell, "The American Family: Some Perspectives," *Psychiatry* 29 (1966): 206.

3. Sandra J. Savignon, "Evaluation of Communicative Competence," 132; Theodore V. Higgs, "Introduction: Language Teaching and the Quest for the Holy Grail," in Higgs, ed., *Teaching for Proficiency, the Organizing Principle*, 6.

4. Office of the Chief, Army Reserve, letter, subject: Accurate Personnel Data Capture on USAR Linguists, October 12, 1984.

Bibliography

Adams, John. *The Works of John Adams, Second President of the United States*. Freeport, N.Y.: Books for Libraries Press, 1969.

American Council on the Teaching of Foreign Languages. "Foreign Language Enrollments in Public Secondary Schools, Fall 1982." *Foreign Language Annals* 17 (1984): 611–623.

Babcock, Colonel Conrad S. "A study of the G-2 difficulties and disadvantages that May Accrue to Blue in an Orange War as a Consequence of Scarcity of Personnel Familiar with Oriental Languages, and Steps that Should Be Taken in Peace-Time to Minimize These Disadvantages." Army War College General Staff Memoranda no. 315 A/44, February 6, 1926. On file in the U.S. Army Military History Institute (hereafter USAMHI), Carlisle Barracks, Pa.

Bailey, Gerald C. *The Utilization of Foreign Languages in Naval Psychological Operations*. Report HSR-RR-66/9As. McLean, Va.: Human Sciences Research, Inc., 1964.

Bathurst, Captain Robert B. "The Patterns of Naval Analysis." *Naval War College Review* (November 1974), 16–27.

Benseler, David P., and Bernhardt, Elizabeth Buchter." Foreign Languages and Global Studies: A Position Paper." Prepared for the American Association of Colleges for Teacher Education. Columbus, Ohio: Ohio State University, 1985.

Bentley, Eric, ed. *Thirty Years of Treason: Excerpts from Hearings Before the House Committee on Un-American Activities, 1938–1968*. New York: Viking Press, 1971.

Bladey, Stephen C. *Approaches to Foreign Document Translation.* Professional Study no. 4075. Maxwell Air Force Base, Ala.: Air War College, 1970.

Blanchard, General George S. "Language Interoperability – A Key for Increased Effectiveness in NATO." *Military Review* 58, no. 10 (1978): 58–63.

Booth, Ken. *Strategy and Ethnocentrism.* New York: Holmes and Meier, 1979.

Brod, Richard I., ed. *Language Study for the 1980s: Reports of the MLA-ACLS Task Forces.* New York: Modern Language Association (MLA), 1980.

______. and Devens, Monica S. "Foreign Language Enrollments in U.S. Institutions of Higher Education – Fall 1983," *ADFL Bulletin* 16, no. 2 (1985): 57–63.

Carroll, John B.; Clark, John L. D.; Edwards, Thomas M.; and Handrick, Fannie A. *The Foreign Language Attainments of Foreign Language Majors in the Senior Year: A Survey Conducted in U.S. Colleges and Universities.* Cambridge, Mass.: Harvard University Graduate School of Education, 1967.

Chief of Staff, U.S. Army. Memorandum for the Secretary of War, subject: Serious Personnel Shortages, February 10, 1944.

Clausewitz, Carl von. *Vom Kriege.* eds. Wolfgang Pickert and Wilhelm Ritter von Schramm. Munich: Rowohlt, 1963.

Cocke, Captain H. C. "Brief History of the Office of Naval Intelligence." Typescript (microfilm MIC A-14A). Washington, D.C.: Department of the Navy, 1930.

Coleman, Algernon. *The Teaching of Modern Foreign Languages in The United States: A Report Prepared for the Modern Language Study.* New York: Macmillan, 1929.

Coles, Harry L., and Weinberg, Albert K. *Civil Affairs: Soldiers Become Governors.* United States Army in World War II, Special Studies. Washington, D.C.: Office of the Chief, Military History (hereafter OCMH), 1964.

Collins, Brigadier General James Lawton, Jr. See Larsen, Stanley Robert.

Conway, Major General T. J. to Brigadier General Henry C. Newton, February 18, 1963. On file among the Henry C. Newton papers, USAMHI, Carlisle Barracks, Pa.

Cummings, Commander D. E. "Oriental Language Personnel." Army War College General Staff Memoranda no. 315 A/44, February 6, 1926. On file in USAMHI, Carlisle Barracks, Pa.

Curricula Branch, Army School Division, Army Service Forces. "A History of the Army Specialized Training Program from its Beginning to 31 December 1944." Typescript 3-4.1A/AA. Also Supplement to June 30, 1945. Washington, D.C.: OCMH, 1945. Originally secret, declassified 1945.

Defense Language Institute, Foreign Language Center. *Annual Program Review*. February 10–12, 1982. Presidio of Monterey, Calif.: Defense Language Institute, 1982.

______. "Suggested Topics for Discussion by the President's Commission on Foreign Language and International Studies." Typescript, 1978.

Department of Languages, The Army Service Schools. *Language Notes and A Brief History of the English, French, German, and Spanish Languages*. Ft. Leavenworth, Kans.: Army Service Schools Press, 1917.

DelCamp, Major Adrian L. "Foreign Language Instruction in Officer Career Schooling." Typescript N8224.194. Ft. Leavenworth, Kans.: U.S. Army Command and General Staff College (hereafter CGSC), 1967.

Druener, Lieutenant Colonel Hanz K. *The Case for Foreign Language Study*. Carlisle Barracks, Pa.: U.S. Army War College (hereafter USAWC), 1968. Student thesis.

Ferguson, Charles A., and Heath, Shirley Brice, eds. *Language in the USA*. New York: Cambridge University Press, 1981.

Fetters, William B., and Owings, Jeffrey A. "High School and Beyond: Tabulation – Foreign Language Course Taking by 1980 High School Sophomores who Graduated in 1982." LSB 84-4-16. Washington, D.C.: National Center for Education Statistics, 1984.

Fiks, Alfred I., and McCrary, John W. *Some Language Aspects of the U.S. Advisory Role in South Vietnam*. AD 434 056. Alexandria, Va.: Human Resources Research Organization, 1963.

Fishel, Wesley R., and Hausrath, Alfred H. *Language Problems of the U.S. Army during Hostilities in Korea*. Chevy Chase, Md.: Operations Research Office (ORO). The Johns Hopkins University, 1958. Originally secret, declassified May 15, 1961.

Fishman, Joshua A.; Nahirny, Vladimir C.; Hofman, John E.; and Hayden, Robert G., eds. *Language Loyalty in the United States:*

The Maintenance and Perpetuation of Non-English Mother Tongues by American Ethnic and Religious Groups. The Hague: Mouton and Co., 1966.

Fox, Major William. "Inter-Allied Co-operation during Combat Operations in Korea." *History of the Korean War*, Vol. 3. On microfilm (reel A141), the typescript is considered vol. 1. Washington, D.C.: OCMH, n.d., originally secret, declassified 1975.

Freed, Barbara F. "Establishing Proficiency-Based Language Requirements." *ADFL Bulletin* 13, no. 2 (1981): 6–12.

______. and Lambert, Richard D., eds. *The Loss of Language Skills.* Rowley, Mass.: Newbury House, 1982.

General Accounting Office. *Improvement Needed in Language Training and Assignment for U.S. Personnel Overseas.* ID-76-19. Washington, D.C.: GAO, 1976.

______. *More Competence in Foreign Languages Needed by Federal Personnel Working Overseas.* ID-80-31. Washington, D.C.: GAO, 1980.

______. *The Need to Improve Foreign Language Training Programs and Assignments for DoD Personnel.* ID-76-73. Washington, D.C.: GAO, 1976.

______. *Need to Improve Language Training Programs and Assignments for U.S. Government Personnel.* B-176049. Washington, D.C.: GAO, 1973.

______. *Weaknesses in the Resident Training System of Defense Language Institute Affect the Quality of Trained Linguists.* GAO/PFCD-82-22. Washington, D.C.: GAO, 1982.

General Headquarters, American Expeditionary Forces (AEF). "Provisional Intelligence Manual, A.E.F." Washington, D.C.: Office of the Chief of Staff, War Department, 1918. Mimeographed typescript, originally confidential, declassified 1949.

______. General Orders no. 30, France, February 13, 1919.

General Staff College. Langres, 1918. Bound, mimeographed notes.

Graham, W. R. *A Survey of Military Assistance Advisors.* Alexandria, Va.: Human Resources Research Organization, 1972.

Hammond, Sandra B. *Survey of Foreign Language Enrollments in Public Secondary School, Fall 1978.* New York: American Council on the Teaching of Foreign Languages (ACTFL), 1980.

Harbord, Major General James G. *The American Army in France, 1917–1919.* Boston: Little, Brown, 1936.

______. *Leaves from a War Diary.* New York: Dodd, Mead and Co., 1931.

Hatfield, Deborah H.; Johnson, Dora E.; and Gage, William W. *A Survey of Materials for the Study of the Uncommonly Taught Languages: Supplement, 1976–81*. Educational Resources Information Center (ERIC) ED 228 863, 1984.

Hausrath, Alfred H. See Fishel, Wesley R.

Headquarters, American E[xpeditionary] F[orces] University. *The Catalogue*. Beaune, France: AEF University, 1919.

Herslow, Nina Greer, and Dersham, James F. *Foreign Language Enrollments in Institutions of Higher Education, Fall 1965*. New York: MLA.

Hicks, Major Harold J. "An Analysis of Foreign Language Training for Officers of the U.S. Army." Typescript N8224.798. Ft. Leavenworth, Kans.: CGSC, 1973.

Higgs, Theodore V., ed. *Teaching for Proficiency, the Organizing Principle*. (ACTFL) Foreign Language Education Series. Lincolnwood, Ill.: National Textbook Co., 1984.

Historical Division, Department of the Army. *United States Army in the World War, 1917–1919*. Vol. 3. Washington, D.C.: GPO, 1948.

Hixson, Lieutenant Colonel John, and Cooling, Benjamin Franklin. *Combined Operations in Peace and War*. Carlisle Barracks, Pa.: USAMHI, 1982.

Holbrook, Major James R. "Foreign Languages and US Army Officers." Washington, D.C.: Office of the Chief of Staff, U.S. Army, 1978.

Inman, Admiral Bobby R. "Language Capability in the Intelligence Community." Statement before the Subcommittee on Postsecondary Education, Committee on Education and Labor, U.S. House of Representatives, typescript, July 15, 1981.

Intelligence Division, War Department General Staff. "Training History of the Military Intelligence Service Language School." Typescript 2-2B/AA. Washington, D.C.: OCMH, 1949.

Johnson, Dora, et al. *A Survey of Materials for the Study of the Uncommonly Taught Languages*. Arlington, Va.: Center for Applied Linguistics, 1976–1977. Also available through ERIC: ED 130 537, 132 883-885, 132 860.

Jones, Colonel William P. "Language Training for the Officer Corps." Army War College, 1960. Student thesis.

Kennedy, John F. Memorandum for the Secretary of Defense, February 15, 1963. Copy on file among the papers of Brigadier General Henry C. Newton, USAMHI, Carlisle Barracks, Pa.

Kissinger, Henry A. See Stolzenbach, C. Darwin.

Kobata, Major Katsuji. "Special Action Force Language Training." Typescript N8224.63. Ft. Leavenworth, Kans.: CGSC, 1966.

Lambert, Richard D. See Freed, Barbara.

______, with Barber, Elinor G.; Jordan, Eleanor; Merrill, Margaret B.; and Twarog, Leon I. *Beyond Growth: The Next Stage in Language and Area Studies.* Washington, D.C.: Association of American Universities, 1984.

Larkin, Major General Richard X. Testimony before the Subcommittee on Postsecondary Education, Education and Labor Committee, U.S. House of Representatives, July 15, 1981. Untitled typescript.

Larsen, Lieutenant General Stanley Robert, and Collins, Brigadier General James Lawton, Jr. *Allied Participation in Vietnam.* Washington, D.C.: Department of the Army, 1975.

Levitt, Jesse. "French as a World Language." *Geolinguistics* 5 (1979): 55–68.

Liskin-Gasparro, Judith E. "The ACTFL Proficiency Guidelines: A Historical Perspective." *Teaching for Proficiency, the Organizing Principle*, Theodore V. Higgs, ed. ACTFL Foreign Language Education Series. Lincolnwood, Ill.: National Textbook Co., 1984, pp. 11–42.

Long, Percy W. "The Modern Language Association of America in World War II." *PMLA: Proceedings* 64 (1948): 645–678.

Marcum, Captain P. C., and Montgomery, Captain K. V. "Foreign Area Officer Trip Report: *Bundeswehr.*" Typescript, 1978.

Matthew, Captain Robert John. *Language and Area Studies in the Armed Services: Their Future Significance.* Commission on Implication of Armed Services Educational Programs. Washington, D.C.: American Council on Education, 1947.

Military Intelligence Division, General Staff. *Provisional Combat Intelligence Manual.* Washington, D.C.: War Department, 1918. Originally confidential, declassified 1949.

Modern Language Association. *Reports of Surveys and Studies in the Teaching of Modern Foreign Languages.* New York: MLA, 1961.

Müller, Kurt E. "Foreign Language Enrollments in U.S. Institutions of Higher Education – Fall 1980." *ADFL Bulletin* 13, no. 2 (1981): 31–36.

______. "The Distribution of Language Enrollments in Two- and Four-Year Institutions of Higher Education in the United

States." *ADFL Bulletin* 13, no. 3 (1982): 5–12.

______. "The Military Significance of Language Competence." *Military Review* 61 (1981): 30–41; "On the Military Significance of Language Competence." *Modern Language Journal* 65 (1981): 361–370.

Muller, Siegfried H. *The World's Living Languages: Basic Facts of Their Structure, Kinship, Location, and Number of Speakers.* New York: Ungar, 1964.

Newton, Brigadier General Henry C. Papers on file in USAMHI, Carlisle Barracks, Pa.

Office of the Assistant Secretary of Defense (Manpower). *Officer Education Study.* Vol. 2. Washington, D.C.: Department of Defense, 1966.

Office of the Assistant Secretary of Defense (Manpower, Reserve Affairs and Logistics). "Foreign Language Training in the Department of Defense." Typescript, 1979.

Office of the Chief, Army Reserve. Letter, subject: Accurate Personnel Data Capture on USAR Linguists, October 12, 1984.

Office of the Chief of Military History. "History of Military Government Training." Typescript 4-4.4A/AA. Washington, D.C.: OCMH, 1945.

______. "History of Military Training, Army Specialized Training Program, Army Service Forces, from its Beginning to 31 December 1944, with Supplement to 30 June 1945." Typescript 3-4.1A/AA, vol. 1. Washington, D.C.: OCMH, 1945. Originally confidential, declassified 1945.

Office of the Chief of Staff, U.S. Army, Study Group for the Review of Education and Training for Officers. *Review of Education and Training for Officers* (RETO). 5 vols. Washington, D.C.: Department of the Army, 1978.

Office of the Deputy Chief of Staff for Operations and Plans. *Review of Education and Training for Officers Implementation Plan.* Washington, D.C.: Department of the Army, 1979.

Office of the Deputy Chief of Staff for Personnel. *Army Linguist Personnel Study.* 5 vols. Washington, D.C.: Department of the Army, 1976.

______. "Language Training for Officers." Staff study. Typescript, 1959.

Packard, Captain W. H. *History of U.S. Naval Intelligence* (title unclassified), 2 vols. Washington, D.C.: Department of the Navy, 1978. Secret.

Parker, William R. *The National Interest and Foreign Languages.* 3rd ed. Department of State Publication 7324. Washington, D.C.: GPO, 1962.

Peers, Major General William R. "Subversion's Continuing Challenge." *Army* (November 1965), 68–71, 136.

Pei, Mario A. *Languages for War and Peace.* 2nd ed. New York: Vanni, 1945.

Personnel Management Development Directorate, U.S. Army Military Personnel Center. "Survey Estimate of Proficiency Testing and Utilization of Male Officers in Foreign Languages." DAPC-PMP Report 58-73-E.

______. "Survey Estimate of Proficiency Testing and Utilization of Enlisted Men in Foreign Languages." DAPC-PMP Report 57-73-E.

Point, Colonel Will H. "The G-2 Difficulties and Di[s]advantages That May Accrue to Blue in an Orange War, by Reason of the Scarcity of Personnel Familiar with Oriental Languages, *and* the Steps that Should be Taken in Peace-Time to Minimize Blue's Disadvantages." Army War College General Staff Memoranda No. 315 A/44, February 6, 1926. On file in USAMHI, Carlisle Barracks, Pa.

President's Commission on Foreign Language and International Studies. *Strength through Wisdom: A Critique of U.S. Capability.* Washington, D.C.: GPO, 1979.

______. *President's Commission on Foreign Language and International Studies: Background Papers and Studies.* Washington, D.C.: GPO, 1979.

Provost Marshal General's Office. "History of Military Government Training." 4 vols. Typescript 4-4DA. Washington, D.C.: OCMH, 1945. Originally secret, declassified 1945.

______. "History of Military Government Training covering the Period 1 July to 31 December 1945." Typescript 4-4DB. Washington, D.C.: OCMH, 1945. Originally secret, declassified 1945.

Report of the Department of the Army Board to Review Army Officer Schools. Vol. 1. Washington, D.C.: Department of the Army, 1966.

RETO. See Office of the Chief of Staff, U.S. Army.

Riccardelli, Major Richard. "Electronic Warfare in WWII." *Army Communicator* (Winter 1985), 40–49.

Ruchti, James R. "The United States Government Requirements for Foreign Languages." In *President's Commission . . . Back-*

ground Papers and Studies, 197–220. Abridged reprint in *ADFL Bulletin* 11, no. 3 (1980): 6–11.

Savignon, Sandra J. "Evaluation of Communicative Competence: The ACTFL Provisional Proficiency Guidelines." *Modern Language Journal* 69 (1985): 129–134.

Schedule for 1930–1931, First-Year Course, The Command and General Staff School. Ft. Leavenworth, Kans.: Command and General Staff School Press, 1930.

Shockey, Lieutenant Colonel Cyrus R. *Language Training for the Officer Corps – An Appraisal*. (title unclassified) Carlisle Barracks, Pa.: USAWC, 1960. Student thesis. Secret.

Simon, Paul. *The Tongue-Tied American: Confronting the Foreign Language Crisis*. New York: Continuum, 1980.

Sinaiko, H. Wallace. *Foreign Language Training: An Investigation of Research and Development for Vietnam*. Study S-232. AD 632 916. Arlington, Va.: Institute for Defense Analyses, 1966.

Sollenberger, Howard E. "Development and Current Use of the FSI Oral Interview Test." *Direct Testing of Speaking Proficiency: Theory and Application*. John L. D. Clark, ed. Proceedings of a Two-Day Conference conducted by Educational Testing Service in cooperation with the U.S. Interagency Language Round Table and the Georgetown University Round Table on Languages and Linguistics. Princeton, N.J.: Educational Testing Service, 1978, pp. 1–12.

Special Staff, U.S. Army. "History of Training – Military Government." Typescript 4-4CE. Washington, D.C.: OCMH, n.d. Originally secret, now unclassified.

Stokes, Anson Phelps, ed. *Educational Plans for the Army Abroad*. New York: Association Press, 1918.

Stolzenbach, C. Darwin, and Kissinger, Henry A. *Civil Affairs in Korea, 1950–1951*. ORO Report T-184. Chevy Chase, Md.: Operations Research Office, The Johns Hopkins University, 1952. Originally secret, declassified 1974.

Strategic Studies Institute, U.S. Army War College. *Non-NATO Contributions to Coalition Warfare*, vol. 1, Basic Report. Carlisle Barracks, Pa.: USAWC, 1981.

Sullivan, Commander John F. *The Language Weapon: Usefulness and Readiness*. Carlisle Barracks, Pa.: USAWC, 1966. Student thesis.

Swenson, Colonel Richard W. "So You Want to Communicate? The

Case for Foreign Language." Carlisle Barracks, Pa.: USAWC, 1968. Student paper.

Task Force on Intelligence Activities, Commission on Organization of the Executive Branch of the Government. *National Security Organization: A Report with Recommendations.* Washington, D.C.: GPO, 1949.

———. *Report on Intelligence Activities in the Federal Government.* Washington, D.C.: GPO, 1955.

Troche, Major Alfonso. "The Foreign Language Area Officer Program/Reserve Component: A Career Program." Typescript (c. 1978).

Truxal, Lieutenant Colonel William J. *A Concept for Language Training.* Carlisle Barracks, Pa.: USAWC, 1963. Student thesis.

U.S. Army, Europe, and Seventh Army. *Exercise Crested Eagle 80: Lessons Learned* (Title unclassified) Heidelberg: U.S. Army, Europe and Seventh Army, 1980. Secret.

U.S. House of Representatives, Committee on Foreign Affairs. *Language Training for Foreign Aid Personnel.* 86th Congress, 1st Sess. Washington, D.C.: GPO, 1959.

Wallis, Lieutenant Colonel Charles R. "Maintenance of Advanced Language Skills in the Army Language Program." Typescript N8224.246. Ft. Leavenworth, Kans.: CGSC, 1967.

Walters, Vernon A. *Silent Missions.* Garden City, New York: Doubleday, 1978.

Watkins, Lieutenant Colonel Norman C. "Cost Effectiveness of Military Language Proficiency." Carlisle Barracks, Pa.: USAWC, 1968. Student Paper. On file in USAMHI.

White, Colonel Wolfred K. "Interpreter – or Filter?" Carlisle Barracks, Pa.: USAWC, 1966. Student paper.

Wilkins, Colonel Wallace W., Jr. "You Are What You Say." Carlisle Barracks, Pa.: USAWC, 1967. Student paper.

Wilson, Major Alexander. "The G-2 Difficulties and Disadvantages that May Accrue to Blue in an Orange War as a Consequence of Scarcity of Personnel Familiar with Oriental Languages; and Steps that Should Be Taken in Peace-Time to Minimize These Disadvantages." Army War College General Staff Memoranda No. 315 A/44, February 6, 1926. On file in USAMHI, Carlisle Barracks, Pa.

The Washington Papers

Currently Available

No.

118 *The Sino-Vietnamese Territorial Dispute*, Pao-min Chang
117 *Spain: Studies in Political Security*, Joyce Lasky Shub and Raymond Carr, eds.
116 *The New Russian Nationalism*, John Dunlop
115 *Romania: 40 Years (1944–1984)*, Vlad Georgescu, ed.
114 *Lebanon: The Politics of Revolving Doors*, Wadi D. Haddad
113 *Negotiating from Strength: Leverage in U.S.-Soviet Arms Control*, Robert J. Einhorn
112 *China's Foreign Policy Toward the Third World*, Lillian Craig Harris
111 *The Soviet Union, Eastern Europe, and the New International Economic Order*, Christopher Coker
110 *Turkey's Political Crisis: Background, Perspectives, Prospects*, Lucille W. Pevsner
109 *Toward European Economic Recovery in the 1980s: Report to the European Parliament*, Michel Albert and James Ball
108 *Jordan: The Impact of Social Change on the Role of the Tribes*, Paul A. Jureidini and R. D. McLaurin
107 *Strategic Implications of the Continental-Maritime Debate*, Keith A. Dunn and William O. Staudenmaier
106 *West German Foreign Policy: The Domestic Setting*, Gebhard Schweigler
105 *U.S. Intelligence: Evolution and Anatomy*, Mark M. Lowenthal
104 *Caribbean Basin Security*, Thomas H. Moorer and Georges A. Fauriol
103 *Small Nuclear Forces*, Rodney W. Jones
102 *Poland: The Role of the Press in Political Change*, Madeleine Korbel Albright
101 *The USSR and Sub-Saharan Africa in the 1980s*, David E. Albright
100 *Looking Forward, Looking Back: A Decade of World Politics*, Walter Laqueur, ed.
99 *The PLO and the Politics of Survival*, Aaron David Miller
98 *U.S. Interests in Africa*, Helen Kitchen
97 *The Politics of Economic Policy: France 1974–1982*, Volkmar Lauber
96 *NATO Burden-Sharing: Risks and Opportunities*, James R. Golden
95 *The Enduring Entente: Sino-Pakistani Relations 1960–1980*, Yaacov Vertzberger
94 *The Future of Conflict: U.S. Interests*, William J. Taylor, Jr.
93 *Soviet Strategy in Latin America*, Robert S. Leiken
92 *The Iran-Iraq War: Islam Embattled*, Stephen R. Grummon
91 *Presidential Control of Foreign Policy: Management or Mishap?*, Robert E. Hunter
90 *Soviet Energy and Western Europe*, Angela E. Stent
89 *Saudi Arabian Modernization: The Impact of Change on Stability*, John A. Shaw and David E. Long